Evolving Reality
Of
Bewitched

AnnaMarie Antoski

ISBN-13: 978-0-9868844-1-2

DEDICATION

Ciara, Christina, Kelsy , Colby, Callum and Christian

And to all the fans of the popular series Bewitched show.
To the fans that are curious enough to expand the Bewitched show into
your natural evolving nature.

CONTENTS

Acknowledgments

Disclaimer :
The information in this book and the author holds no responsibility for your own choices for medical attention, assistance or medication or any other practices mentioned.

ACKNOWLEDGMENTS

The love and enjoyment of the popular series Bewitched and how it dazzled to fascinate us with humor and expand our minds to an evolution of empowerment.

AnnaMarie Antoski

For all of us that are fans of the famous series Bewitched show,
it spans the test of time through all the years since it's original airing on television.
The Bewitched show
can still amuse, enlighten us with humor and fun.
Best of all it can expand our consciousness to curiosity of the possibilities that await our future to experience.

AnnaMarie Antoski

CRAFT 1

++++++++++++

BEWITCHING QUANTUM PHYSICS

Presently to date there are unlimited numbers of experiments that have been performed repeatedly just for the reason that they all seem to show such impossible things become possible. I am sure that you would agree that it was inevitable that science eventually had to come to this expansion to show what all ancients masters have known all along. It's part of our spiritual evolution to expand our consciousness to experience heaven finally on earth.

Or when we perceive it from a Bewitching point of view, that will finally allow Samantha to use her powers without Darrin continuously interfering. However we do know that Samantha has the choice, she is only allowing Darrin to control her because he is the one who is a little scared to step completely out of the box of the norm.

We have been like Darrin for too long hypnotized into limited beliefs that strip us of any power. Since you are reading this book you may either be curious or have chosen to now become more like Samantha.

We must become to realize that we are more then our physical bodies and that there is infinite realities, infinite dimensions. Sure why not just pop it to us all at once, baffles us, excite us, confuse us, but before we know it we eventually become accustom to it and that is what quantum physics has done.

The only way to really be able to comprehend anything that quantum physics shows us is for us to expand to a larger reality. Scientists started to add ten to eleven dimensions until they came upon the realization that infinite dimensions were needed to be able to make sense of quantum states. The old classical ways of science with three and four dimensions just does not fit the new model of quantum mechanics. Just as science always seems to do, start with theories and progresses through experiments to give validity to evidence that they can then label as facts. Mostly for the skeptic minds that have not accepted what ancient wisdom and masters always knew.

Quantum physics has been showing us things that appear so magical because what other labeling words do we have in our limiting minds to try to comprehend it all?

The majority of the population for all of humanity's history has been reacting and thinking more from the rational logical beliefs that has always limited us. And what does that leave us to think? Mostly in closed separated structures of beliefs, like Darrin.

Even though many religions have always believed in more expansive beliefs, many were flavored with dogmatic religious webbing judgments that never allowed us to expand to any powerful potential.

Many of the teachings have been altered or misinterpreted for us to honor anyone or anything more then to honor our own self. Those webbings still blocked the openness of what revealing new experiments and experiences are showing us about our reality.

So we do realize that a small majority, a few wise masters have carried the quantum reality through their cultures. However, very little if nothing at all has ever leaked into the mainstream compared to what quantum physics has done in the past couple of decades. It's shows like Bewitched that not only entertain us but also have deeper meaning for us to wonder about and question reality and our beliefs of what is possible.

Quantum physics allowed many different varieties of rational minded individuals to take a peak into the weird spookiness it had to offer. And experience is always the wisdom because when you observe and experience any of this spooky bewitching stuff, there is no denial when you see the evidence for your own self.

So let us take our magic wand and stir up some of that spooky quantum brew and observe what we find. Since there are so many experiments they can be researched and they are wide open for investigating. I am only mentioning the ones that I found exciting for us to know about our reality and how it pertains to our daily lives. Keep in mind that all experiments are prevalent to showing and expanding our comprehension of our reality. Most of us have no concerns or desires to know the mathematics or calculations or the properties of reality from the largest atom to the smallest neutrinos. All we desire is the evidence of what the experiments show us that we can use for creating with awareness of what we want in our daily lives.

Though it is so simple once we stop giving attention by attaching to old thoughts that keep spinning us like Darrin of the reality we no longer want.

The most exuberant fascinating experiment is the **"Observer Effect."** Regardless who is doing any of the experiments what they found was that the individual doing the observing actually affects the outcome of the experiment. It shows that the observer and what's being observed is connected or to expand our minds even further, they are actually one.

Now, I am not a physicist however have studied quantum physics from the best scientists and their books, though they have done all the hard work of the math and equations. I only wanted to know the powerful results. Just as many of you reading this book may also choose to know of only the information from quantum states we can use in our daily lives. We just want to know how we can finally be like the Bewitched family once and for all, to know that its a possibility because if we can think it then its already in the quantum field of potential consciousness to experience. So we can jump into the most interesting stuff, the information of what all the experiments showed as a result, that we can use in our daily lives to make it more magical.

We now know that whatever we are most passionate and excited about is the most important for us to follow because it is the passion that inspires us and leads us to keep on going for more. If we are not passionate about what we want then we will not sustain the inspiration. It's the inspiration that keeps us so ecstatic so that we keep doing whatever we have to do to manifest the experience.

So if you feel the same way as I do and have no passion or interest in the math and equations of quantum physics, that we just want to take the most important parts for our brewing.

For those who are not familiar with the wisdom of creating our own reality you may desire to ponder the idea. For the individuals that do know from all the wisdom we have learned so far is that we create our own reality and it also affects everything else along the way in our experiences. What many of us have come to realize as we are practicing and learning how to create our reality, quantum physics pops in to help us along with scientific data to prove allot of what we have already been practicing and became to know. So now our once rational brain like Darrin's limited beliefs becomes more flexible and accustom to accept these new ideas and now we can have science back it up as evidence.

If you are noticing as I am, that not only are we seeing our own proof from our own experiences, it is popping up in so many ways in everything and everywhere with more speed then ever before in our past. Things we would be burned or beheaded for in the past are now becoming more in the mainstream and accepted, we are evolving in comparison to our past history. So we can appreciate, just like Samantha does, how far we have evolved.

So it is all a part of the quantum brewing going on because we know that whatever we give our attention to, which is what we are observing, we are going to see more of.

We all have had the experiences that if we buy a red car then we will see more red cars everywhere, yet in the past we never noticed so many red cars around. It is because we had no interest in red cars previously, it was not part of our attention until we are interested in a red car and then our attention became our focus on red cars. It is because of our focusing on red cars that we then zoom in to see them everywhere, yet in the past we never realized to notice. Just as Darrin had no knowledge or experiences of seeing or knowing witches until he met Samantha, now his life is filled with witches, warlocks of the Bewitching family. So science is the same way, it makes sense that science would see the proof of what we have been doing all our lives because finally they are expanding. In the old science they were not aware of the nature of reality and no attention was on newer ways until more desires started surfacing and quantum properties starting popping up.

The more we observe the more energy we give it, the more we focus our attention on it and this is the "observer effect" the genie of the observer effecting reality. So whatever we observe long enough the more it will respond instantly in proportion to our energetic observing of what we expect. It is so finely tuned of a fine line of energy because it seems to take our rational thinking of separate compartmentalized ideas and unite them all into one. We are no longer separate from the observer, we are the observer and the effect, we are connected, we are one, unified and entangled.

Just as a particle is in a solid state until it transforms itself into a wave, which then is a fluid energetic state or vise versa, a wave can become a particle. Is the same as when we have a desire, its in a wave, in a fluid state until we choose our desire and focus upon it with intention, observing it as if it is already physically manifested and then it does. The desired wave becomes a manifested physical particle. That is collapsing the wave of desire into a solid particle, our manifestation experienced in physical.

The physical manifestation becomes into a solid particle state from the once fluid wave of desire. Then like magic, almost like the magic wand or as in Bewitched, the incantation being our focusing of attention to observe it as we want it to become. Then like moving a magic wand back and forth, or using an incantation to keep the focus, as long as we keep observing it in our mind focusing on it as it is already created, it eventually becomes manifested into physical.

Quantum physics is just showing us what we are already doing and have been doing throughout humanity the only difference is we did not know we were doing it. We were unaware of what we were doing all of the time on a daily basis, creating reality from what we focused through observing that affected the outcome to expect what we receive as our manifestation. Quantum physics came along to speed up the process as evidence especially for the rational brain mind thinkers to move their skeptical minds to expand and this is the nature of reality and how it has always worked. Just as Samantha came along into Darrin's life to show him what other realities are really available that he did not see previously in his life.

Experiments using photons in a solid particle state and then while being observed changed properties into a wave length functional state. With only a few clicks of your fingers you can now via internet watch video's showing all of these experiments. It has been just over the last couple of decades that technology now not only allows us to read about everything that is going on in the world and experiments but to also view by watching videos. So quickly we have advanced to bring so much data and information to everyone world wide, everywhere. We are evolving finally in expanding consciousness collective planetary mass then ever before.

I am not going to go into long detailed information about every experiment done because if you are interested you can search it out so easily now. For many reading this book you are probably already in tune with all of this, its prehistoric stuff, but for anyone not yet informed, there is no more excuses, its all available quickly to find if you desire.

Let us tune into just a fraction of individuals who have paved the way for us in explaining quantum states. The physicist Michio Kaku and in his books, "Hyperspace" and "Physics of the Impossible," with great information, analogies containing many of the experiments and more. All of Gregg Braden's books and work give detailed explanations of experiments that also relate to our ever day lives.

Bruce Lipton is another amazing teacher of information too with his experiments and experiences in biology. Ramtha communicated through J.Z. Knight is amazing because his teachings not only explain all the quantum information but also brings us to the leading edge to do what Ramtha teaches with practiced disciplines. When we experiment by practicing new empowering ways to experience the proof that will expands us to becoming our powerful beings in physical.

The "observer effect" is a beneficial experiment that gives us the evidence that whatever we are observing we are effecting the physical matter in magical ways. This is exactly what we are doing when we think and choose unlimited thoughts from higher or infinite consciousness.

When we focus on something long enough, which is being the observer, we are affecting our reality. On a daily basis we may be affecting the reality in ways we do not want, like Darrin, because of old automatic habits from beliefs that continuously keep us on that path. It is until we come to notice by being aware of not only what we are observing but how we are observing that will create the expectation we expect. It's by being aware we then can control and be present in the powerful present moment so we can progress to fine tune our observing effect consciously. Then we are deliberate in the way we create our reality to be instead of just thinking that everything just happens to us as Darrin believes when he is under a spell.

To know the only spell we are under is our own conditioned beliefs that is always creating our reality and might also be limiting the desires we want. When we become wiser and aware of how it works this gives us power to change anything we desire or want by observing it the way we expect it to be manifested and created as a result.

It is important to remember that what we choose to think is like a burning fire that continues to expand more thoughts to more thoughts of the same. For an example if we have a belief that has a bunch of thoughts attached to it that automatically dictates us to believe that if we get rejected from another person then we feel hurt. We do not have to feel hurt, we just feel hurt because we have attached other thoughts and feelings to an already hurt belief, fear belief of thoughts of memories. Rejection in itself has no meaning, it is all dependant on what we have valued as a belief that will create an automatic reaction, then more thoughts of what we attach to it is what we believe rejection should feel like.

Now what if we took that neutral perception of rejection and believed that it is a mirror reflection back to our own self? Then we have attached rejection to be a learning tool to expand into knowing more about our self. Maybe the rejection occurred because we seem to reject our self in many different areas of our own life. Everything always does show us our own reflection, we can hide behind denial for as long as we want, eventually and especially if you are on the expanding evolving path you will desire to face these denials. To be able to expand to see the whole picture through the experience to see the tool that is reflecting of what we believe rejection has the power to do to us.

Denial is the trick that fools us to believe it has to be felt in a hurtful manner which is only an old habitual way of believing to think about it. Just like Darrin always seems to take it when Endora puts a spell on him. Darrin perceives in his mirror reflection that Endora is trying to aggravate him. And of course many times we can see that Endora does enjoy aggravating Darrin but Darrin could also perceive it as a great learning experience for himself. Oh I know that's what kept all those years of episodes running but since we are observing it from a higher consciousness perception we are going deeper into reality.

So rejection is the tool, but the power is not in the tool. Its in what we attach or choose to think of what we believe that the tool is allowing to reflect back to our self. Of what we may be rejecting in our own life that it attracts through law of attraction or in the reflection from another.

Can you realize now that rejection is only what we choose to think it to be?

A neutral observation is where all the power is when we observe it that way. It always depends on how we choose to observe it. The old way of reacting from rejection is to feel hurt which then creates feelings of sadness and maybe further expansion of depression because you believe you were not accepted for yourself. This is what happens to Darrin everyday in his life too.

Do you really accept you own self in every area of your life?

When we make the switch we are then able to feel differently about being rejected and instead we look at it as a very positive experience that then expands to more positive expansions. We can be thankful for the rejection because we did not realize we still had it in us to work on. Then we look to see what needs to be changed, maybe you are rejecting your self from doing what you really want to do with your life or career. Or maybe you are rejecting your own self love, do you really love yourself and accept yourself? Again we cannot lie to our own mirrors and everyone and everything that comes into our life is there because we put out the energy, the messages from our own self to begin with. Its always a mirror reflecting back to our self about our self and also a ripple effect of our future experiences too.

It is always the observer observing and then depending on how we are observing that's effecting the creation of the outcome, depression or elation?

It's how you choose to observe all experiences that is the most important part to be aware of. It is always returning to fine tune our own self, so its a learning curve to become more of what we want to mirror out and see in our own reflection of experiences. When we then respond differently then we did in the past to rejection or anything that is limiting our self, then we are changing our reality bit by bit.

So we can take any limiting belief and transform it by observing it in its neutral state so we can then respond differently which will create different outcomes too.

Let's take a look at another experiment. Researchers used a volunteer, swiped DNA from his mouth and put his DNA into a vacuumed empty container, then moved the container to another room in the building. The researchers stimulated the volunteer with emotional stimulation by showing him videos that triggered reactions of joy, compassion, fear and anger. What the researchers found was the volunteer's DNA that was in another room reacted instantaneously to his emotions as if they were still connected to him, but they were not as he was in a separate room from his DNA. As they continued the experiment by moving his DNA over 400 miles away from the volunteer and received the same reactions instantaneously. Then many other experiments followed with farther distances even to other countries from where the volunteer and his DNA were separated and all experiments showed the same results.

There is no denying it. All the evidence has shown regardless of how apart the volunteer's DNA was from him the results were the same. So not only does it show us that we can effect our DNA that is separated from us but also that there is no traveling time either, its instantaneous. The observer being the volunteer affected his DNA miles away with no rational connection but an intelligent field that most now refer to as Source, or God, or the quantum field, the gap, the zone, point zero, vortex, there are so many labeling names for it, but its one infinite source. The infinite source is showing us that everything is connected through this QUANTUM FIELD and is affected by the way we think then feel, in how we react or respond whether in fear or anger or in joy or happiness or love.

The most amazing part of the experiment is that there was no traveling time, something very challenging for our rational beliefs to accept. The volunteer's reactions were instantly received. That changed everything because rational logical idea's influence many to believe that to get anywhere it takes traveling time, yet these experiments were showing us the opposite.

There is no traveling time, its instantly received, instantly.

This information in itself shows us the most incredible evidence that our reality is much more fluid and connected then we believed. It breaks apart our beliefs about linear time and makes it appear to be more bewitching then ever. Which is what Samantha's family does all the time. They can pop in and out of anywhere to anywhere they desire and they are always popping in literally to see Samantha and the kids. They are observing what they desire and through their observation affecting their reality instantaneously. They live the quantum life of teleporting and it makes everything easier and more fun then living the old way of traveling and manifesting.

So what does that mean for us in our daily lives?

It changes everything in the way we perceive linear time.

It shows us the infinite possibilities of what our future can become and also gives us more evidence of how fluid time is in space.

We all have experienced how time flies by when we do what we love to do compared to doing things we do not enjoy as the time seems to go by so slowly. That in itself shows us how fluid time really is. By acknowledging this in our daily lives by doing more of what we love to do actually changes how we experience time in our spacious momentum of our lives. We have perpetually heard the phrase, "do what you love to do and money will flow" becomes to make more sense when we see it from the quantum states.

We individually affect how our time will fluctuate in how we choose to live each day, it can be a heavenly life or a dreaded life, the choice is always up to our own selves when we know it. And that changes everything.

How Stress Affects our Body

Now let us take a deeper look into evidence of stress on our bodies and how it can affect our lives. We already have so much evidence available in the mainstream that shows us that stress which is a fear feeling effects our bodies. By releasing chemicals through our bodies that either constrict our cells body flow or in a relaxed state allows the cells of the body to flow in great harmony.

It is in the restriction that causes diseases which stops the flow of harmony in our body. Just as bending a water hose, we know when we bend it we then stop the water from flowing, when we release the restriction the water then flows easily. Which is the same within our bodies with restriction from choosing thoughts to be stressful compared to unrestricted thoughts which allows the flow.

Many experiments were done that actually showed the body's reactions to restriction with stressful thoughts and feelings and a relaxed body when loving, compassionate, joyful feelings were felt.

They have observed brain waves changing from emotions, blood flow, and many other parts of our body with all the technological advances that are now accessible to observe our bodies.

We can do our own experiments just by putting our focus in the moment on our own self. Think something dreadful and feel the reactions in your own body. If you stay focused to feel the sensations you will feel your body tightened in certain areas. You will notice that its harder to breathe, your muscles eventually get sore, till eventually you feel pain and shortness of breath.

Now do the opposite, focus and think of something that is so loving, that is so joyfully exciting or blissful and feel the difference in your body. You will then notice your body starting to relax, easy to breathe, to move, no stiffness, no aches or pains, you feel light.

Our body is always communicating to us what we are in the feeling of when we attune ourselves to feel, take notice of what it is telling us through communication of pain or no pain. We can feel it in parts of our body that is affected. If you believe that when another rejects you and you feel heart broken about it, you really are affecting your heart which becomes restricted from the pain and then the flow is disrupted. Everything starts internally with what you choose to decide about what rejection should feel like. If you are not consciously choosing then you are reacting from the old automatic beliefs, but you are always affecting your body by what you are thinking and feeling.

We can see the comparisons between Samantha and Darrin. Darrin is always stressed out with all that is going on in his life but Samantha keeps a peaceful relaxed state no matter what is going on.

When we shift to create rejection or any stressful experience as a good thing like Samantha would do and use it as a learning tool our body stays in harmony.

This information shows us that it can be exciting because prior to that we were not aware of the meaning we gave everything that then created our reactions. Instead when we become self aware and change the meaning so that we respond peaceful and relaxed that will be beneficial to our body. Now we get a different process which then gives a different result. We feel good even when we experience something stressful and we perceive it in a beneficial way, then our body is feeling good too. There is no restriction just a continued relaxed feeling in your body which keeps its natural harmonious body flow through all your body cells.

If you choose to believe that there is a reason for everything that seems to just happen, that will also be a benefit, it's a positive energy too. When we take all disempowering thoughts that create the disempowering feelings to something, we are changing from the old way of thinking to a new relaxed way of thinking that creates a relaxed feeling. These better feelings creates different cascades of proteins compared to the stress thoughts that changes the chemical reactions in your body therefore creating healthier results.

The new way expands you to grow and continue learning more about your self which changes everything on the new path. Your body still feels loving and good and you change also as a result and so does your future. For one you won't have any body disharmony and instead have a harmonious body of cells that creates your body to be and sustains it's health. Until the next person or situation you will attract to show you more of what is really inside of yourself.

We will always attract to us of the energy we put out that brings another to us in any encounter. When we know this and are aware of it then we create all situations and experiences to harmonize our thoughts, to feel good to create health all of the time. We benefit from learning and growing to expand to know more about ourselves and we also benefit with our health at the same time.

More informative specific information about our body and its effect from our emotions, beliefs and thoughts can be researched from Bruce Lipton. He is a biologist who has found all the proof anyone would need to convince one self of this truth. Our DNA can be changed by the way we respond to our environment and everything we interact with.

This is so beneficial because we become to create a future in alignment with what we want instead of what we may not want. And continue to observe it with the deliberate observation of expecting it as the end result. All of this becomes a result of just deciding and choosing a more powerful enhanced thought that then creates the healthy feelings that allows the process to continues to unfold. This is how we can realize that we are expanding to become to know more because we come to realize that it has always been our own self doing the choosing and creating to begin with. Maybe we should explain this to Darrin too. When we live this way for ourselves, we become a better role model for others, so if Darrin chooses to change he can too.

Self Healing without Dr. Bombay

As for the Bewitched family that still has a doctor, Dr. Bombay, even though he portrays quite the comical and most outrageous prescriptions. I know we can also eliminate even the doctors in our new evolving reality. How do I know? I know because for over twenty years I have not went to a doctor or used medication

When I came across Seth, channeled by Jane Roberts and Louise Hay's books that go in such detail of information on healing our self. I delved so passionately into it, literally. Rereading their books and turning to the books especially Louise Hay's little blue book every time I had any illness or pain.

Then I took it a step further by introducing self healing to my sons when they were younger too, Louise Hay's books were always on my coffee table for quick reference. I even bought over twenty books and gave them out to everyone in hopes that they would also be so passionate in knowing their own bodies and heal themselves. Whether they did or not was not my concern, just that if they choose to they had the resource to do so. For me I continued to grow and trust myself completely, I can not even imagine allowing anyone else, especially any medical person to tell me what I can only know of my own body's communication.

I must admit many times I do call my father as he grew up on a farm and knew nothing other then their own trusting of healing and their bodies. Though once he was subjected to the city life and medical assistance he did semi conform to it. However he still heals so many parts on his body that is so magical to watch the quickness of his healings.

My mother well she had a great mantra she lived by which I must admit was a great affirmation for me to learn through being around her which was, "I have no time for sickness, I am just too busy!"

So through their role modeling and beliefs they have helped me on my path of becoming sovereign in healing my body and health. However on the whole they have conformed to taking pills which I gave up twenty years ago, no medication, no doctors, only me and my body communicating to me what I need to know to bring it back to its natural harmonious flow of balance. So sorry Dr. Bombay in my evolving bewitching enfolding life I will have to say so long to you, however still enjoy your humor.

So we have come to a realization that everyone has free will to choose whatever they want to believe about the impossible becoming possible. There is no more use for denial unless one chooses to stay in denial because there is evidence everywhere now to prove the impossible being possible.

Quantum physics shows us the proof through experiments and other individuals on the planet that are doing so many things that seemed so impossible yet they are doing it. But of course the most essential evidence is when we experience it for our own self and then can do what seemed impossible. And continue to practice and do more to make anything we thought was not possible to become possible through our own experiences. Then we can use the Bewitching family as role models to evolve into those types of experiences for ourselves. What a magnificent fantastic life we then are able to live.

CRAFT 2

+++++++++++++

DEEPER INTO THE PARANORMAL

Wikipedia's definition of the **paranormal**, "A general term to describe unusual experiences that lack a scientific explanation, or phenomena that alleged to be outside of science's current ability to explain or measure." We can clearly see this description is already out dated because it is not taken into consideration any quantum science into its context of describing.

Quantum physics sparks factual proof for many skeptics of the paranormal. Trying to bridge the skeptics to expand their minds and brains to believe through spectacular evidence the experiments show. Which might even convince Gladys, remember the episode when she caught Samantha rearranging the pictures on the wall? Gladys started to experiment on her powerful self and was really getting into it until Darrin and her husband didn't think it was a very good idea. Though we may never be able to convince her husband Abner of any bewitching powers because he is just too skeptical and close minded. This episode portrayed Gladys's desire and passionate excitement in practicing witchcraft, however she allowed the others to persuade her and then she finally gave it up. If she continued to practice and sustained her belief in herself and whatever it took until she was able to experience her powerful abilities, she would of evolved farther. However she allowed the others to detour her and she was left to continue just observing through the Bewitched family. Leaving her in confusion to never really know if all she was seeing was true or not, even though her intuition was urging her to the truth.

If we look into the crystal ball, as quantum physics does we know that everything changes and we can see it naturally in nature. But if we take it for granted we will miss the opportunity to learn from nature. It shows us everything when we take a long enough observation. It will show us the evidence that is captured in nature that we can use in the comparison to our selves through changes.

Since I have moved to the country with nature spread out for miles I have learned so much from nature. My mate and I had planted many trees in the summer they seemed so fragile and innocent in the new surroundings and environment. We planted them in the wide open fields with nothing to protect them but their own strength, as there is only fields stretching for miles. Sure wish I had Endora around as she would of planted the trees with the wave of her hands and it would be done, she was my greatest role as nothing would alter her from what she wanted to do.

It was great in the warm summer but when the season changed and the winds became strong and so cold I wondered if they could withstand so much pressure. The fierce cold winds blew steady for days without releasing its strength and I would sit and watch with such wonder of their strength. How the trees held so strong with their roots firmly in the ground, yet flexible enough to blow so wildly for days in that cold wind. Realizing that it was a result of the fierce wind that actually strengthen them to grab their roots more firmly in the ground. Though I did know it was part of their growth I would still worry if the trees would make it? I also realized my own reflection as soon as I even posed the question as I am always working the observer effect and mirror reflection back to me. I realized that since I was going through many windy turbulent challenges in my own life, I was perceiving with that invisible filtering lens my own fears, would I be able to withstand these challenges. Would I be knocked down into fear and depression through all these challenges, am I still that weak and frail to think they can knock me down?

I became aware of how I am so much like those trees, the challenges are expanding me to grow and learn about the nature of reality. That no matter what I am going through, I can be like those trees perceiving everything as an opportunity to learn from and expand my mind to more knowledge. If I believe I am that frail then those trees since they are in my reality of perception will just be pulled out from the storms and perpetual winds. Through my observing perception I would remind myself how the winds actually create the trees to become strong through the trees own challenges. So when I used the trees as my own mirror reflecting back to me of what I was perceiving I realized I knew it in a rational intellectual level, yet in my rooted beliefs I still believed I was still rooted in so much doubt, fear and undeserving beliefs. Similar to Aunt Clara when she messes so much up with her spells that don't turn out as she desires them to.

That was the real eye opener, the real awareness of my belief that was still there popping in and out guiding me to more thoughts like that to create more low vibration feelings of uncertainty. Yet I thought I knew I create my reality, I just did not realize how deep these rooted beliefs were and how they were continually creating what I did not want, all the challenges. Yet it was the challenges that created me to reflect to know what my hidden beliefs really were that were dictating my life. What a paradox everything became, until I started to really sit in the eye of the storm to be so aware to know more. Most importantly to realize and stop reacting in the same old limiting ways to experiences in my life and instead to respond with love and trust which then would shift my energy to deserving.

To come to the knowledge that everything I could perceive around me were my own creations, everything. Grown from my old beliefs, old expectations that were continuously creating some experiences I did want and other things I did want. Yet my infinite self knew of these creations and that they would expand me to always go further to learn more about the nature of reality. So when you look at whatever challenges you are going through you can be quite sure they are all opportunities that can allow you to expand to know more about yourself and your own reality.

We can also look at the trees and we know that underneath the ground the roots of the trees span in such large areas, continuously growing under the ground. If we use the analogy of the tree and compare it to our own self as the tree and our beliefs as the roots under ground that are not so easily to see that are really creating our lives. Also how deeply rooted many of our beliefs are from years of living from their guidance. It is similar to trying to pull out one belief at a time when we start to go through changes from learning about ourselves and the nature of reality. Exactly what everyone is talking about in reference to the movie "The Secret" and what was left out of the movie for it to work effectively which is the beliefs. Because no matter how much we think about a desire, if our beliefs don't support the desire then we are way out of alignment with manifesting or receiving it. It is until we can get into the believing stages of our desire that we come closer in synch to the vibration to manifesting it.

The trees they can also teach us longevity. The chirping birds regardless of the weather extremes will joyfully eat and enjoy their day. I have put out bird food and watched them enjoy it even through the fierce blowing cold wind and snow, they still are chirping and eating regardless of the weather. I watch as they glide with the wind, they seem to create fun out of everything. It showed me that I can take all situations and experiences and not allow it to alter my bliss as I did in the past.

Just as observing the water of small rivers freezing into solid form in the cold winter and thawing into a flowing wave when it thaws from the warm atmosphere that engulfs it. Is similar in showing us from many experiments in quantum physics as solid particles transform into waves of energy. And how we can be that flexible with our perceptions.

All we have to do is take a glass of fluid water and freeze it and it's properties change from one form to a different state of a frozen ice cube. Then if we put the ice cube into a warm environment as a stove burner on high it will not only melt from its solid form of particles into a liquid form and then into a boiling steam that is evaporating into the air. One physical object transforming in front of our eyes from a solid state of properties then transform into another state of properties, fluid and then into another state of properties steam, all in a few minutes. This can show us how we change depending on what we believe and react to those beliefs and the different outcomes we then create.

When we get to the paranormal stuff as in the Bewitched series everything is paranormal depending on how we perceive it. The trees can be paranormal when we observe them that way. The tree we see with its trunk, branches and leaves is what we normally see objectively. Yet if we envision what is invisible to us of the inner landscape we could perceive that the invisible under the ground is there even though we don't see it until we were to dig it up. So in that sense then the tree could be perceived as paranormal.

If we were skeptics like Abner about the reality of the paranormal and then desire to know more about the nature of reality as Gladys seems to border on then we need to learn all we can about it. We may need to dig through those old limiting beliefs so newer expanded beliefs can support the idea of the paranormal. Depending how deep they are and how passionately desirable they are to you will make all the difference in how much time it takes.

So science was invented to go deeper to explain to understand what nature and reality is, what the universe is, and how we can know how we are a part of it. Yet science is so behind from the ancient masters who have always known.

What is regarded as paranormal is telepathy, telekinesis, remote viewing, teleportation, psychometrist which is picking up information from objects, levitating, out of body, channeling, time travel, levitation, aliens, UFO's, clairvoyance, ESP extra sensory perception, manifesting out of what seems thin air, premonition and anything that is perceived out of the normal abilities. Do keep in mind the para of paranormal is all dependent on our evolving to just know more about what is commonly perceived as not normal. The more that we experience and see the underlining functions of it then we become to see it very normal, like the bewitching family does. To Darrin the paranormal keeps him from becoming more like his wife Samantha and her family.

Now let us dissect the paranormal into more specifics of their functioning in our everyday lives.

Telepathy

Telepathy is our nature and it's our natural ability of picking up or tuning into thoughts from others. Without realizing it, we do it all of the time. If you think of someone and shortly after they called you on the phone that is telepathy, either the other person tuned in on your thoughts or you picked up on their thoughts, either way you connected by the medium of the phone. Whether we are sending or receiving thoughts via whatever technology we are using, it's a medium for our transferring of thoughts energetically.

When Samantha calls her mother verbally, we can hear her voice ringing in our own minds, "Mother where are you? Appear right now!" That is also what is occurring, her mother Endora picks up on Samantha's thought message, telepathy and then pops into her reality by teleporting. You think of a friend and then like magic within a few minutes they call you. It is when we observe what is really going on and not miss out on the it is showing us that we are doing to not over looked the potential for the awareness of telepathy.

Quantum experiments have already proven it when they send photons in opposite directions and regardless on how far the photons travel apart does not matter. The other photon has the other photons information even before it is sent traveling apart from each other, actually they pick it up instantaneously. There is no traveling or time gaps, it is absolutely instantaneous. It is the same as I explained with the volunteer and his DNA being separated yet instantaneously his DNA instantly knows whatever stimulation he experienced.

Remote Viewing and Out of Body

Now what if that friend you thought of for a few moments just popped into your kitchen, it would really freak you out, yet it is being done though remote viewing, except without the physical body. We could travel through our minds intention to the friend's home and read the book they are reading, then call them to confirm by reading the few sentences to them. Or whatever they are doing we could observe and then call them to confirm if we were right or not, that would of course be the proof. We can perform many of the quantum experiments ourselves by practicing it and getting our own results.

Many rational minded individuals do not like that idea because that is an invasion of privacy, who wants someone to be an invisible peeping tom? However, if we see it in the light of Bewitched, we can realize that when all of us use these powers we can also know when another is in the room. That of course is also the advantage of owning our own powers too. But until then we can use these types of experiments with permission and with integrity only for the purpose of experimenting to confirm to ourselves that it is possible. With our intention being for knowing ourselves and capabilities to experience of using more of our brain and DNA to evolve, that would take on a different vibe and intention to it. Which also comes into play that "whatever we put out we get back" so that takes care of any karma lingering.

We must take into consideration that we do it all of the time anyway, we are just not aware that we are doing it because we have never been aware of most of our thoughts on a daily basis, so we assume that this is not occurring when it is. If we were to know and observe what is going on behind the illusions of our rational beliefs of reality, then we would realize that we are always traveling as out of body with our thoughts and picking up on everything. But if we are not aware of what is really going on then we are not able to confirm any validation of it then we are never wise to its truth. Realizing that we are doing it all of the time because we are always choosing more then 70,000 thoughts a day, we are doing it all of the time, just not aware that we are doing it.

Really think about this knowledge that whatever you are putting your focused concentrated thoughts upon is where you attention is, is where you really are literally. Your body may still be sitting there doing what it naturally does to keep you going, but your mind is off somewhere else, and that is where you really are.

When we sleep and dream it is going on, however when we awake we either do not remember our dreams and if we do we just pass it on to it being nothing insignificant unless we become aware and connect the dots. In our dreams, we are totally focused in another dimension of reality, while we are in our dreams we feel physical until we awaken. We are doing the same thing if we are daydreaming, imagining or focusing our attention on anything, we are traveling but not in physical, we are in other dimensions. The difference is that we have these labels of perception from limiting beliefs that give us a fractional speck to perceive that narrows our understanding of these other dimensions.

Let's delve into telekinesis.

Telekinesis

Telekinesis is the ability to move objects with our mind or energy, which our mind is energy, everything is, so I will refer to it as our mind.

In the beginning of the first season of Bewitched the first episode when Samantha is trying to convince Darrin that she is a witch, she moves the ashtray back and forth. There are so many individuals already doing this on our planet, if anyone cares to research it on the internet and I have gone into depth about in another crafting chapter. Of course the best way to know of its truth is to be able to practice and do it personally our self.

For me I have been able to bend a spoon over an inch without touching it and only using my energy and intention. So I am still practicing this and many more disciplines to further expand my knowledge into my own proof for myself. That is the best undeniable wisdom, when you can do it yourself, who can tell you it is not true? You know it because you can do it. Since anyone can do it shows the proof that it is possible. To go even beyond that knowing, if we can think it then it is already a possibility because we have picked up the idea of the thought from the quantum soup or infinite consciousness the field of infinite possibilities.

When we can actually do it and experience telekinesis, what we are doing is expanding from our limited belief into an expanded knowing to break free from the limits of the normal perception into a new perception. In other words we have recreated a new belief that will support the new experiences or desired manifestations. We are really becoming one with the object we are moving because all of our focus and attention is zoomed into that one frame of reference. To become one with anything and tap into its data of information is to fine tune our focus onto the attention of one thing, which is moving that object to experience it.

The linear time it takes is dependant on the individual and their own beliefs. For me it took a couple of days and hours of practice with visualizing already doing it and holding my hand and pressing on the seeming invisible air of energy around me and the spoon. Which really is not invisible because anything we perceive as invisible really does have energy. For some they can do it in shorter time or it may take longer. It depends on each individual and their own belief systems that show us our own levels of acceptance and how it can change with each successful experience.

It is exuberant feedback to show our selves just how hard core and stubborn some of these limited beliefs really are and to observe to know through the transformation of them. All paranormal comes down to energy, since everything is energy it is tapping into the knowledge turned into wisdom of it by the experiences for one's own self.

As we can observe when we watch any Bewitched program they are so proficient at it, it is so natural to them because they were born into those unlimited beliefs to begin with. Though we do have these divine inherited abilities, our beliefs are limited until we create the new empowering beliefs to support the empowerment.

Teleportation

Let us expand some thought of teleporting. What a wild way to travel, to just pop into anywhere we wanted to go. Time would collapse into more space because we would not need all the traveling time as we do now, which really seems quite prehistoric to teleporting. Of course we would have to stop being like Darrin and be able to pop to a friends home or any location that we desired to go to. No matter how many times Darrin preaches to Samantha not to use witchcraft, even he becomes tempted and asks for witchcraft to be used when he really needs it.

In the episode when Darrin becomes obsessed in his desire to stop Larry from breaking his leg in the future. We can see that he really seems to enjoy the use of Samantha's powers to help him out. It saves magnificent amounts of time to be able to pop from one country to another in a second. So even though Darrin does seem to be hypocritical much of the time Samantha doesn't seem to mind because she just loves him so unconditionally.

Teleporting in our future would save on fuel and the use of needing vehicles. By eliminating all the traveling time we would condense all that time we have in our space which would leave us to do even more adventurous things.

It is our linear seeming continuity that gives our perception that time is slowed down to the momentum of broken frames of our reality being separate from the true timeless spacious void.

Let's use the analogy of dial up server for our internet provider and the amount of time it takes to download something? It's so slow in comparison to the high speed server of cable or fiber optics. To download a video on a dial up server takes hours and after all that download it usually disconnects making it almost impossible to do or too frustrating to perpetuate the trying of it. Compared to cable or fiber optics that allows a few seconds to download just like magic could be how we travel now compared to teleporting.

In the Bewitched show's reality, it shows us so clearly the differences of how we live life now compared to living it the bewitching way that is so empowering, simple once mastered and effortless.

Endora loves Paris and is always asking Samantha to pop over with her to some shopping, with the waves of their hands, they are enjoying an hour in Paris until they pop back home. Darrin would not be any wiser to what was going on, unless what usually occurs something is left as evidence to show that Samantha was not home.

Though it may sound outrageous to the rational mind, quantum experiments have shown the proof. Our future may evolve to teleporting and surely it will change the way we live now. When we collapse more of our linear time that we are using of our space, things then would change very rapidly on all levels. Just as our past history before vehicles were created, it was horse and buggy for traveling. Look at the difference in time traveling between a horse and buggy compared to a vehicle then compared to a plane. Back in the day if we were to tell our ancestors that we would one day in the future travel by plane they would not be able to comprehend it either. Just as many skeptic minds still cannot comprehend teleporting now. We first must expand our minds to accept all possibilities as an idea before we even realize it so we can be living it.

Now let us take a deeper look at premonition.

Premonition

I love it when Endora so nonchalantly tells Samantha that Darrin is walking through the door before Samantha even realizes it because she is so focused on trying to figure out how to get herself our of trouble with some kind of explanation. She is preoccupied and not aware to pick up on that future moment that Darrin is about to walk through the door. Samantha's rational thinking is getting in the way of her tapping into the present powerful moment of focus as Endora is using as she peeks into the quantum field.

Premonition is the ability to see the future before it arrives. From a linear standpoint or perception where everything seems fragmented and in frames, as in comparison to the old slides of a film to a video cassette is a good analogy. When we merge the slides to be shown onto a video without any fragments it is viewed without the broken up separated compartments that the framing does for slides. And on a video tape we can fast forward near the end or stop within any part of the video we want. It is more organized then slides because the slides are separate. When we expand the analogy further from a video to a DVD we even have more flexibility and less effort to find a frame we desire to perceive. With the use of chapters contained in the DVD we can easily pick a chapter we want compared to a video where we must fast forward of rewind that takes more time.

Reality is the same way depending on what we view in our experiences as we are perceiving it. Just as viewing our earth from the moon changes the perception compared to viewing it from the ground on earth is so different. From the moon the earth looks like a speck of a spot, just a round small ball. Edgar Mitchell the astronaut stated while he was on the moon and looked at the earth, he could put his thumb over his view of earth. Now how mind expanding is that? What a difference of perception from how huge we perceive it on the ground. It seems so massive yet to the astronauts the could see it no bigger then their thumb. It is all in the perspective of how we perceiving to view everything. This is similar with reality when viewed from linear it just seems so massive yet if viewed from a higher plateau it is no longer linear but happening all at once. And that makes all the difference because then we can view it in no time but as a momentum of energetic frequencies of waves.

We must also consider we have free will and the appearing distant future we can grasp, however its quite fluid as it can change with any different choice that is made. Just as if you are driving on a trip to one location to another and have your destination yet if you detour you will take different roads. The different roads may lead you to a variety of different experiences yet you will arrive at the same destination. Unless you change your mind and decide to go somewhere completely different then your original destination, in the moment you changed your future of your original destination. Reality is more like that because of free will. What may have appeared to be a future result changes its path and a different future then results from the change. However if we are viewing it from a higher plateau it is easier to get a grasp of the whole changes taken place. Instead of waiting for a phone call from you who took the trip to say that you are no longer at your original destination. If I were on a plane and monitoring your journey I would already be seeing the changes taken place and the path that will unfold to your chosen new destination.

So if we view premonition that way then we can get a better intuitive for how it is unfolding and pick up data to be known of the probable future, yet we are able to see the next moments of the future even easier because it is in closer proximity. We have to get into the focus that allows us to gather the information from the quantum field or infinite consciousness because that is where there is no linear perceptions. In the quantum field there is only now and everything going on simultaneously, infinite dimensional realities, there we can zoom in by our focus and get the information we desire.

Let us go a bit further into the paranormal of manifesting something from what appears to be thin air.

Instant Materialization Manifestation

Instant manifesting or materialization is not really coming out of thin air, it is coming from what we are still perceiving as invisible. So for the invisible to become visible, we must synch into the unified variable vibrational frequency of the object we want to manifest.

Through the illusion of linear limited perception it appears as if we manifested out of thin air because that is what the linear beliefs have been conditioned to support and perceive. It takes massive expansion evolved knowledge to comprehend the understanding how quantum physics works and what our world is really made up of. Without that knowledge it would just appear as spooky and may be confusing of how it could be even possible for another to manifest an object out of what illusionary appears as nothing.

When we become to understand the quantum states and all the seeming magical ways quantum states behaves then we have more of a stable grounding to understanding its nature. That's the reason that an indidual can manifest from what appears to the linear mind as nothing or air because of the quantum field of all possibilities. When we get into the quantum states we can pull an object from one variable vibrational frequency to another just like appearing as magic. Behind the illusion of magic it is really quantum science facts beyond this limited three and four dimensional reality. So the truth of it behind the illusion is that we are through our focus and attention creating the properties of an object and fueling it with our focus to materialize it into our physical frequency. It comes from another dimensional reality, out of the infinite quantum field of infinite consciousness.

It is logical that if we needed a loaf of bread that we would have to go to the store and purchase it with money. Then we bring it home and we have our loaf of bread, we had to travel to get it. That is the linear slowed down way that the norm get things that they want. That is logical because it is what we have been doing for so long that it is a natural way to get it. Or we could bake a loaf of bread then we would not have to travel or purchase it or even leave our home. Those choices are so linear and habitual in the norm of the every day linear way of doing things and is the way that Darrin wants Samantha to live. But if Darrin was instead an open minded scientist or psychic researcher instead of his job in advertising he would probably be more open to bewitching. Because quantum physics and his own observations of research would show him that there is no traveling time in the experiments that are all done with success. Why would Darrin insist on doing it the same old way? Except for of course the Bewitched show creates quite a fantastic series. In true reality I am quite sure that if Darrin was open to bewitching then he also would prefer to live a more effortless life.

When Samantha wants something she does not have or something she needs to cook with she just zaps into her reality, magically the bewitching way. The same as a few individuals are doing now however we are not aware of them, they are like the red car we used as an analogy in the previous chapter. It is when we are interested and diligently focus our attention that will lead us to the information we need or do more research on it. But it will always be from our own personal experiences that we will know if its possible or not. Whether we see another manifest instantly or experience it our self. Instead of getting a loaf of bread the old way wouldn't you prefer the new way? If it was possible and you were able to learn to manifest a loaf of bread into your reality the new bewitching way through your focus of energy, what would you really prefer? Humanity can stay prehistoric as Gladys and not pursue these greater abilities and just sit in the denial sidelines believing its impossible or too outrageous. Leaving it up to the leading edge masterful individuals who are breaking the ground and evolving their abilities for our future generations.

Depending on our level of what we accept as truth through our beliefs we will then experience it in the amount of time we expect it to manifest. If we were to be daring enough to consider these abilities and even extend our belief to consider what it would do for our future. For our first loaf of bread to materialize to manifest may take years of practice to manifest it, however if we practice it and do it over and over we will become to master the ability. Just as any other skill we practice long enough until we become to do. We will then come to accept our own evidence for our self because we then have manifested the object and know it is something anyone else can do also if they desire to. Then we do not have to travel the old way as in classical science we then can work in quantum states of getting what we want. We then evolve into living a bewitching life literally, not only evolving to live it but actually become to live it daily with the new fantastic experiences. Which of course makes everything in our life faster, easier and effortless. We would no longer consider it as magical or para of the paranormal but then normal because the illusions would be dissolved and new beliefs were created to now to support it.

With those abilities we would have much more time to work on other exciting new adventures to experience. Who would not be intrigued to live life that way compared to the old linear way that takes too much time in comparison to the quantum living. The comparison would be like Darrin compared to Endora.

CRAFT 3

++++++++++++

PEAKING INTO THE QUANTUM CRYSTAL BALL

Let's see just how imaginative we can be as we concoct in imagining some wild ideas that we would do if we were just as powerful as the bewitched family. Or as powerful as many masters who are already using many of these ideas and experiencing a magical life. We would probably refer to these beings as super beings.

When we have important data of information that is essential to grasp and know from quantum states that allows us to expand our minds further to try to comprehend some of these ideas that may sound outrageousness. Yet it is only outrageous until we comprehended the impossible into possible as a belief of truth. Once that knowledge has grown to expand into wisdom then it's not so out of the ordinary, especially when others are doing some of it already. But for the ideas that pop up that seem too extraordinary then we must realize that when we think any thought, any idea it is already in the quantum crystal ball or in the infinite dimensions of consciousness. How could we think it if it has not already been thought or done? Any thought or idea we come up with no matter how impossible it seems to this physical reality, is already there in that quantum state of possibilities or we would not have been able to think it. When we really absorb this information as great wisdom then nothing, absolutely nothing is impossible. So let us go into some of these ideas with that type of perception to really get the grasp of it all.

If you have given some thoughts about teleporting, telepathy, channeling, telekinesis, extrasensory perceptions, remote viewing, and bending metal with only your mind, let's take a breath here. Maybe you have also thought about what it would be like to walk through walls. Yes, you read that correctly. These are very creative ideas yet are already being done by individuals on our planet. What? You may react but yes, there are others doing it whether you believe it or not does not mean it's not being experienced.

Even though the above list may seem long there will always be new abilities to add to it as we choose from the infinite dimensions of consciousness. When we connect with higher selves or sources of beings from the infinite consciousness it becomes more helpful for us. And if you still do not believe that there are others who are experiencing these outrageous abilities it may take loads of research or actually seeing another do it. For now let us use this chapter to really stimulate your open mindedness to expand into the infinite brew of possibilities.

Have you thought about flying with our physical body? Oh I am sure you have, I can feel that all of you that are reading these pages are quite a wild bunch. Together we are so wild that we know and feel the presence of each other in the room. So whether you are here with me sharing this space somewhere in time as I am writing or maybe you are deep asleep and dreaming that you are watching someone typing away at 3 o'clock in the morning.? Or maybe you are out of body traveling around or maybe you are just thinking about writing in some sense. Or maybe your invisible spiritual you is experiencing yourself as letters themselves. The possibilities are infinite in how everything can be connecting.

You are reading this in a future time from when it is finished and published. Yet you can get a feel of a sense of my time now because the energy of these letters into words on the pages of this book is all stored energy. That energy can be tuned into to pick up any time. It can be fun to ponder these ideas around for a bit so it can bring us into the powerful energy that is around us. When we are ready we can then tune into that appearing invisible until we open ourselves to take notice.

As we expand more on the idea of teleporting if it was possible with our physical body it would be fun and create our lives to be effortless in comparison to traveling as we do now. We would just pop ourselves into where we wanted to be just as the bewitching family. But to be able to physically fly as Bewitch does, like a bird or even a plane so high above, to be able to experience what we would see and feel during the flight would be quite an amazing experience. I am sure eventually since so many other impossibilities are being done now that we will become to be able to one day also do this too. Just as flying as traveling in a plane seemed impossible until it became discovered and perfected. Try to imagine life without the discovery of planes now? That seems just as impossible considering the majority of everyone traveling by plane, its quicker and saves time. We can already hover like a bird with specific gear that accommodates us, however I mean without anything but our energy, mind and body.

I used to wonder about this idea for years and maybe you have too? To discover and invent a machine similar to vision telephone on a big screen TV. And through the machine we could call to connect to all of our departed loved ones that passed through what we refer to as death. Imagine the possibilities!

We could call up our deceased aunt and connect through the line and both of our physical appearances would appear in real time on the screen. Similar to the workings of how video Skype is used now. My aunt could tell me what she is doing in her reality and I could tell her what is going on in my reality, while simultaneously we could see each other in real time on video too.

Let's continue to imagine that a month went by in my linear perception even though her time perception in space may be an hour in comparison to mine. But if she decided to incarnate back into my physical reality when I called her, her messaging machine would say in her voice that she is no longer available. It would explain that she has incarnated back to my reality and I could now call another number and reach her. Of course once the invisible veils of illusion were lifted we wouldn't need these types of machines to communicate because we'd become to master it, but for now we will focus on the machines. So the message would continue, but give it a few years to be able to continue to converse because she would be reborn as a newborn. Unless we became mastered at walk ins into other bodies. However past incarnations of realities would still be available in our memory banks to retrieve. Maybe we could retrieve them like speed dial list just as we now have on our phones. Or if we contacted another relative who passed on through death and choose a different experience as going to another reality plane of existence, then we would get that message. This would be the thinning of the veil of our realities, like opening a door to other realities in more a physical expanded ways.

We could have gadgets or app's as we have on cell phones now. It would show us on a screen of other beings that are around us but presently we don't see because our beliefs are still too limited in our perception. It would be similar when we get the feeling there is someone else in the room. We could get our new flashlight and by shining the light in the room where the invisible beings are located that we don't see the flashlight would illuminate to make them appear visible to us. We'd be our own ghost busters and even surpassed Samantha who usually asks her mother if she in the room when Samantha gets that feeling. Or if another being wants their presence to be known by us our flashlight would give a signal just as a ringing of our phones. This would alert us and we could then illuminate them for our communication or visitation.

When it comes to our heath, most of us by now, myself included already do not need Dr. Bombay because we became our own authority a long time ago. Well if you have not yet then it may still be one of your desires. Even though Dr. Bombay was advanced for his day with that pitch rod that he would put against Samantha's body. This resonance rod would not only show what we need to heal but also to instantly heal it with its vibrational resonance. Vibration resonance is bringing our natural body cells back into alignment so that the cells can function with ease. It is when we disturb the orchestrated rhythm of our natural well state that disease becomes created as a result. Which is no longer resonating with our natural harmony state of being. Presently we know doctors do have these types of rods similar to Dr. Bombay as lazar devices to disintegrate gull stones. Also available and used is a device that is so small yet can be inserted into the body and travel through the body showing up through e-x-rays. I just heard about a pill that can be taken that has a small camera and can do the same thing. We are advancing slowly but surely we are evolving to many technological ways and eventually we will evolve in natural ways too.

Let's continue to ponder more ideas.

Let us imagine If we wanted to visit the relative who passed on through death but let's say they have decided to incarnated to another planet of reality, we could just pop in there without even a space ship.   Just like Samantha and her family just pop into wherever they want to go, not just of this earth but of parallel earths and any other dimensional reality that we choose. When infinite is available there is nothing then that we cannot visit. Though it may be a bit challenge for us to imagine what infinite really is like, just the little sparks of it is so expanding to imagine.

Just trying to imagine how this new future world could be as a result of all these possible ideas and how it would alter everything as it is now. Just imagine what it would be like? It also follows in the aligning flow of a peaceful world because anything of a rational egotistic way will not be sustained in this new world with all the new powers. That in itself leaves you with a infinite imagining of possibilities. So if your mind is stirring in more possibilities, feel free to share it on my website under the Infinite Possibilities page.

CRAFT 4

+++++++++++++

SPELLS & INCANTATIONS AS AFFIRMATIONS

What are spells and incantations?

Spells and incantations are either rhyming or non rhyming words that propel powerful intentions to direct the energy to manifest what we want or desire. Does that sound familiar? It sure does! I am sounding a bit like Darrin here who is always asking and answering his own questions before Samantha even has a chance. Though most of the time in the show Bewitched it gives Samantha time to come up with a good explanation to tell Darrin about anything that has gone on. Her puzzling look leaves such an impression in our memory of her.

We can realize that affirmations is what we refer to as a label to define what we use today of what magical spells and incantations were in the past, in alignment with Bewitched. Referring to spells and incantations just gives the sounding of it a more magical mysterious vibe but they are the same identical things or tools to use for manifesting to create the reality we prefer.

Whether we are aware of what we are doing minutely, which most are not, but it is what we are doing and always have been doing infinitely. We are creators creating our personal reality and always adding to mass realities. We are the witches, warlocks and sorcerers just with present day different definitions, yet are doing the same thing mostly without awareness that we are doing it.

Since we are similar because if we were not you would not be reading this book. So we diligently take notice and try to be aware of what we are putting our focus on as much as we possibly can. We realize that there is so much going on minutely its a challenge to be watching every thought that comes along that we may subconsciously be choosing. I have learned that the best way to do this was to start with affirmations. Whether it be by reading evolving books or listening to evolving information on a daily basis is the same as affirming. Affirming is a way of directing our focus to keep us in alignment with that evolving knowledge and is recording all the data of information perpetually every minute into our memory for further use.

So when we desire to evolve what we do is present ourselves with as much new stimulation of the new data to sustain our focus to be more aligned with our wants and desires. Affirmation is a powerful tool, just as spells and incantations are when we do them repetitiously. The only difference is we have gaps in time lapses especially when we begin on this journey of wisdom of knowing we are creators creating. Even though we may desire to be like Tabitha as a child she is able to be so right on, want it then manifest it. We may be more like Aunt Clara that is stumbling with her power because she believes she is becoming less powerful with her deterioration of aging. So we are more in reverse of Aunt Clara, we are learning and stumble because we are practicing to master our powers. When we come to realize that the more we practice with high deserving source esteem we become to get better and better at manifesting. The most important thing here to know is that when we desire something the message is received instantaneously. Immediately and we could be like the Bewitch family and receive our manifested desire immediately. If that is true then what gets in the way of us experiencing it instantly?

Our own selves gets in our own way with any limiting beliefs or expectations that we have regarding the desire to manifest instantly.

So in a way we could be like the family of Bewitched if we could just love ourselves and feel absolutely deserving to receive what we want and desire for our selves. This is where affirmations come in to guide our minds to become more in alignment with our power. If we affirmed or created a spell that states, "I love myself, I accept myself, I know I am a creator creating my reality" and so on. And if we affirmed it to ourselves throughout the day, every day, eventually the affirmation would seed into our memory. Then eventually when an opposite thought comes up to try to create us to doubt we insert the new affirmation to change it to the esteemed loved one.

Let us view it from a different perspective. Let us use an example of another person that we do not get along with or have negative feeling towards and use the example of how Darrin feels about Endora. Many of us at some time in our lives have gone through something similar to what Darrin goes through, dealing with a seeming difficult individual. Our hearts will always try to guide us to forgiveness, to make peace with our self over what we believe about what another is doing that is disturbing us. Usually and eventually we will come to peace with the other person, we will eventually come to forgiveness, if we don't then eventually in some lifetime we will.

Still using Darrin as our example we can put ourselves in his situation through compassion of how he believes it is so challenging to deal with Endora. Whenever Endora pops up into Darrin's thoughts and if he continues to choose by attaching negative thoughts and especially with feeling towards Endora things get messier. We always witness when Darrin becomes angrier Endora puts more energy of a spell into the situation for Darrin to learn his lesson. So Darrin's not forgiving Endora and continuing being in a state of anger at Endora perpetuates more difficulty to deal with. We can perceive this the same way for ourselves when another individual irritates us and we react with more anger feeling disturbed as a result. This is similar with casting a spell because the negative reaction keeps the negative energy going. That spell or negative reaction is loaded with energetic energy of maybe hate, revenge, bitterness and so on, that is a loaded spell of energy. As we come to know that everything is energy, especially our thoughts, we are loading a spell with an energy that will go somewhere. Maybe not even to the other individual that we allowed to upset our self, it could be a total stranger that would tune into the energy.

When we know that energy never dies or discontinues it only transforms. So whether the thought is picked up by the other person that we allowed to upset us, even if they do not pick it up someone who is aligned with that type of belief system will pick up on it. What if they were already feeling low and depressed and that fueled hateful thought feeling was picked up by them and that was the icing on the cake, so to speak, or the loaded spell that pushed them off the edge.

Now this may sound absurd or too outrageous but in the nature of reality of energy it is what it is, the way energy and telepathy works. So would you then take responsibility for that negative spell or thought/feeling you had? How would you even know of the connection if you did not think about it to take any notice that everything is connected? These are very profound powerful questions to ponder.

There is a two fold here because those negative thoughts and feelings you have about another person is also affecting your self too. This is where taking responsibility for your thoughts and feelings is important not only for others who tune into them but also for yourself. Your body cells are listening with feeling to what is going on with your thoughts and feelings so it is effecting the way your body is reacting to it too. So we can look at it as a learning situation to get us to notice what is really going on, which can then transform that awareness to be an opportunity to realize and change our perception. Which then changes our feelings about the other person which then changes the energy dramatically, like a 90 degree turn. Eventually when enough work is done on one's self, then the change will be made. Our perception will be changed from upset or disturbed to forgiveness, which is always returning to a love spell for our self. It expands through consciousness to whoever then picks up the recycled thoughts and feelings. So really every thought and emotion does matter, it is always going somewhere but firstly it is always having an effect on our own selves. This is benefit enought to realize that taking responsibility for our thoughts and feelings is such an evolving awareness for us to continue to do.

So if Darrin would be aware in the beginning and use it as his opportunity to grow into more bewitching ways, he would automatically forgive Endora. As a result there would be less or no more challenging experiences for him to go through. But I know we are glad that he didn't because we enjoyed the show to continue on for as long as it did. Entertained as we watched Darrin perpetually forgive Endora which was a great start that moved him finally out of his anger and frustration which made Samantha very happy.

Now through hindsight we can watch the Bewitched shows with a new perspective that we can learn and grow from as a result. We can also realize that a spell or incantation is really an affirmation and has many benefits already embedded with dynamic energy. An affirmative of what we are thinking and then feeling that is going out to somewhere or someone continuously and effecting our selves too. We realize that spells can be very powerful not just for manifesting what we want but also what we do not want and even to realize where it will go and end up as a result.

If we were to create an affirmation or a spell that states, "I forgive myself, I have returned to being loving" and so on. We then take our power back in many ways and create a better potential for its release for all reasons on all benefits.

So to think of thoughts and feelings as affirmations and spells because they become powerful domino effects and boomerang's effecting so much more when the wisdom comes of its potency and power. This can bring us eventually to the realization of the wisdom to know that no one can really affect our love and bliss unless we allow it. When we allow another to affect our love and bliss, whether aware or not, we are giving our power away, always. When we become aware of this we then can realize that we gain momentum of power back because we use the awareness as an opportunity to work on changing it. If we never take notice of this powerful wisdom to keep returning to our selves then we will spend lifetimes giving away our power to others.

The spells, incantations or affirmations are neutral until we give them the definition that defines what we are going to put out. Instead of letting it be based on automatic reactions going unnoticed to transform it to realizing it by awareness and transforming the thoughts and feelings which are spells, incantations of affirmations all day long.

CRAFT 5

+++++++++++++

LOOK OUT DARRIN HERE WE COME

As I have already mentioned that it is easy for the Bewitched family to not only naturally accept their powers but also do the most seemingly impossible things compared to mortals or us humans. It is their heritage, yet it is our heritage too, we just did not know about it until we became more expanded and wiser by expanding our consciousness to grasp to understand it.

Through other evolved beings we have been guided to the information that we are Creators which is not only similar to the Bewitch family but even more powerful. To really know, to experience being a creator on a daily basis is to own and honor our creative creating god or creator given divine heritage and rites. So Samantha look out because here we come, we are not going to let the others Darrin's in our lives alter our way of our divine powerful heritage.

Though there is quite the difference in saying, "Yes I am a creator" and then if we do not practice it to really experience it for our own selves then it is just merely words. Experience is everything when it comes to taking knowledge and transforming it into our own wisdom into our daily lives to experience what we can do. The more we do the expanded extraordinary things then the more we expand which is evolving the spiritual into the physical. Is that not what our main purpose may be for us to learn and do in these lifetimes? Does it feel so powerful when we can do things that seem impossible in comparison to what the norm mortal does?

So knowing is one thing but when we experience it we have no doubt, no denial, no one can alter our wisdom because we have done it for our selves as the proof. This is where all the once assumed junk DNA was sitting there awaiting activation for, to own our creator hood, our own magical powerful heritage of our own bewitching life. Just look up Gregg Braden as he exuberantly goes into specific detail on this subject, that the god gene was actually found and deciphered in our own bodies. So it is our heritage, and what we have always been doing, creating without knowing we were.

This is when we can tell Samantha that we also own these similar capabilities as she does. For many of us who have awakened to this wisdom, we choose not to let any type of Darrin alter us from our divinity, or creator given heritage.

We unlike Samantha want to use our powers as much as we can because we know with practice we can perfect it and expand it further master it like Samantha. Darrin can be perceived as the individuals in the reality box of limited minds that may still not want to accept this as our reality. That is fine for them and Darrin if that is what they choose. We all have free will but for the ones who do want to expand our creator given power and rites we are also free to. We will be on the leading edge that others can follow as we evolve to the bewitching ways of living life.

So we realize that Darrin lives in the limiting box and is always trying to control Samantha to not use her powers when it is so natural for her. Just as for ourselves when we will not conform to the norm when expanding ourselves is so much fun and part of empowering evolving. We then become like Endora who accepts with honor her magical powerful being and way of living so easily and with so much sparkling magic and miracles. To be on this leading edge, which eventually the collective consciousness will one day evolve for the majority of the population to experience their powerful real natural selves in physical.

So we choose to role model Samantha's parents, her mother Endora and father Maurice. We just want to bring it all on and tell Darrin once and for if he wants to be in the norm that's fine but just leave Samantha and us alone to do what we want. Finally take our own power back just as most of us always wanted to tell Samantha when Darrin got in her way.

The new way of a bewitching divine life and what we are on the leading edge to evolve to become, melting away all those old limiting beliefs that have been valued for too long. Life can then be easy, we do not have to do what we do not love to do. We always have choices, whether the choice is to change careers, partners or just perceive our careers or partners differently. From a magical empowering way to transform everything into joyful love of fulfillment instead of the old dreary way of the past. Bringing passion and inspiration of bliss into everything we perceive and do. That is evolving, that is allowing our magical power to unfold and using the powerful potential of energetic vibrations of frequencies of thought to the highest powers that we can. Take the thoughts we become aware of and transform them to joy, love, all possibilities of empowerment.

Take all thoughts that at first pop up of anything we do not want and transform them into what we do want, all of the time.

A great example is if we are in debt and the bill collectors are calling all day long and all we can see around us is this lack and limitations of what we really do not want. By perpetuating those same disempowering thoughts of emotions we add more energy to get more of the same. It is when we continually transform the thought to the energy of what we want it to be that we empower the thought to become more in the expansive energy of what we want. If we are in debt and cannot find a way out, then we must practice this diligently through out every hour through out each day for the momentum to change its direction. So every time the thought of limits pop up, transform and think of what we'd prefer, over and over until it becomes so natural that those powerful thoughts seem to be more of what we think about. Then the direction of the momentum will follow the new thoughts into the direction we want to go, next thing we will realize our lives are changing, money starts to pop up from everywhere.

This is using our powers in bewitching ways to create what we are giving our energetic attention to by transforming the thoughts to what we'd prefer. That is powerful because in the old way we were creating, however in the opposite direction that we wanted to go. The momentum really builds up in speed giving us more so we can experience the proof for our self of it occurring. This also gives us even more desire to continue to go in that direction with everything because we are evolving into more of what we can be, the magical beings we are.

By going in the opposite direction we then become less of what we are capable of and land up in depression, feeling like a victim with no power, creating in the direction we do not want. Which feels better?

The powerful way!

By continuing in that powerful direction we also will be surprised at all the other experiences that come along on the journey with it.

So Samantha sorry but we think you should divorce Darrin once and for all, just kidding or am I? Of course we know that if she did divorce Darrin then the show would not be what it was intended for our enjoyment. All the contrast created the show to be what it was to stimulate all and everything that it could for the entertainment purposes. For many I am quite sure that the desire of the possibility to join to be like the Bewitched family was stirring and for a good reason too, to evolve us in the process.

CRAFT 6

+++++++++++++

BEWITCHING INSTANT MANIFESTATIONS

Why is it that we are becoming to know that any desire we have is immediately received, just as in Bewitched. Samantha's heritage shows us that when they desire something, anything, instantly so magically it just is. They can with the snap of their fingers or waving of their hands or using spells or incantations just magically create whatever it is they desire whenever they choose, no matter the distance. They can move things, pop things in and out from one location to another, create anything out of thin air, immediately. Once we become to know from our own experiences that we do create all of our reality we will notice that we also create especially at first a lot of what we don't want. We probably also notice that our desires manifest but for most of us it is not instantly.

We will notice a variety of time gaps when we have a desire or wants and sometimes we wait while keeping the focus on our desire as pure as we can. We are learning to trust without doubt that one day it will manifest to us. Yet that one day could take a week, a month, a year or years before we finally receive the manifestation.

For starters we were not born consciously knowing we are creators creating our reality or as Samantha and of her heritage. Samantha had the absolutely knowing from birth that she was a witch and everyone in her family were warlocks and everything else that the enchanting bewitching reality holds. They had no doubts in their beliefs systems, they just knew that is their heritage and they had the power to manifest instantaneously was in their genetics forever.

The difference for us is that when we are born without that powerful wisdom, we were given an altered ego to work with that would guide us and keep us in line with reality. That altered ego guided us to become fearful even though its intention was to protect us and keep us safe. Our ego became stuck in survival mode similar to us having divine amnesia of not being aware of our own divine powers. The doubts, fears, with very little divine self esteem and beliefs that we were not deserving of anything better or were even capable of anything more then mere survival. Which lead us to be stuck in the victim role and the beliefs that things just happen to us and we that we must accept that role which is a continuous spin of being stuck in our lives.

Until some great teachers and masters came along and introduced us to information, knowledge that resonated with us about being more then we thought we were and that changed everything.

To know that we do create all of our reality by what we think and feel and that our environment is our mirror to reflect to know ourselves and what we believe. From that reflection we can then recreate by creating new thoughts that continue to keep us to feel in empowering ways. Which we now know is to evolve, which is to know more and experience more expanded reality then our past experiences.

We are now to the point in humanity in the present with the knowledge of that powerful wisdom of what we really are, creators creating. If it takes us a long time to create what we want it is because we have to perpetually pull ourselves out of all that muck of old beliefs that kept us stuck for so long. Through new experiences we then are breaking old beliefs and creating new ones to support and sustain our new experiences.

We realize that this may have been humanity's destiny to go through the survival, victim path. That it took those survival experiences for us to realize the ancient wisdom, the secret, that only was reserved for a few. So now it is out in the open and compared to the Bewitched heritage, we seem to go backwards from how they were born into what we label "magic" with esteem. We were born thinking we were tainted with sin and had to forgive all our lifetimes and give our power away.

So now we get to the point in humanity where even though it is a small percentage of the population, it is enough to bring the collective whole of our planet to start shifting. Bringing us back to where Samantha started to begin with. Now we go from this point to evolve our selves into the empowerment that we always had but did not know it until we now. Then we must work with it for awhile because we have to bring up new memories for us which is really ancient memories that allows us to know what we can become as a result.

Let us take a closer look at more reasons why we have gaps of time in space lapses in what we desire and the reasons that we are not able to manifest instantly. So we realize that our heritage upon birth did not allow or reinforce those beliefs as in Bewitched. Once we know it our newer beliefs become established from experimenting with the ideas that we are creators, similar to Bewitched, that we do create our reality.

Which moves us from beliefs that created us to be victims into transforming us into powerful creators now in charge of our lives . Once we have seen enough evidence for our own selves that when we desire things we eventually do see them created for our self. Some things seem to take longer then other things but on the whole we do seem to experience it more and more on a daily basis. Enough proof that we now not only believe it, we know it is true, it has become wisdom through our own experiences. Then this is when we come to the point of wondering and desiring to know why there are the time gaps in the different lengths of time we wait to receive. And even though we come to realize and believe that everything could become instantly manifested, we are getting a grasp of the understanding that it is all up to our own self literally.

We see proof of it everywhere when we observe how others can manifest their lives to be so fine tuned with what they desire, financially, in relationships, in making an income from what they love. Yet for many others it is still in the mucky spots of so close but yet so far. It is all dependent on our belief, our self esteem and deservingness. Yet we admit and know that we have been working on all these limiting beliefs for so long and still it is still far away for us to manifest. It could be that instead of taking a quicker route without realizing it we were taking a longer route to get to where we all get to when we become in harmony with it all. It is all dependent on our own levels of acceptance and how much we prove to our own self on a daily basis. For everything we do that we could not do before creates a new memory from the new experiences that become hard wired in our brain. It is the same thing for new skills that we practice long enough to experience our success at it.

To take a quicker route would be for us to forget about trying to bring up all those limiting beliefs that keep reinforcing the old beliefs. Because we are dealing with recycled thoughts in consciousness memories and the list of them can really be endless because we are picking up thoughts from lower frequencies. So we are best to just stop and bring ourselves into the present moment and work for there when we know that this is how our beliefs work. Then make conscious aware choices of thoughts as often as we can throughout out our hours and days. Then we can just work with what we are doing and continue from that by perpetually replacing any old limiting thoughts and feelings that come up. Observe and replace, observe and replace and continue to observe and replace, until it becomes such a daily natural habit and becomes what we do all of the time, automatically. Then we will become to notice that everything starts to flow for us effortlessly. Since we then realize that we pulled ourselves out of the mucky quick sand once and for all and kept the momentum going so that we are then on a new flowing easy path.

Now the long gaps that we did not accept that were in our past become less and less of a gap, they become more fine tuned and aligned in the flow of harmony and of Source, or your higher self that we start to feel so much power. We could compare it to Samantha getting amnesia for awhile and then getting her memories back. Samantha would be like Darrin until she remembered that she had all the magical powers.

We could also take a look at people with multiple personalities because they do it all the time. A person with multiple personalities not only does the same thing as Samantha with amnesia they do it with multiple personalities when they switch from one genetics to another with each different personality they play out. When they change personalities it is also instantly, no waiting, they just change to another personality with that genetic that makes up the personality that they play out.

Yet most of us keep waiting, keep working and trying to get into that flow, to have the gaps of time to become smaller which lessens the time of waiting for our manifestations to be received. When it is all dependant on our levels of accepting whatever it is that we are trying to manifest. Our desire and our manifestation has to be in alignment with each other which means our beliefs have to be in that pure acceptance level to actually surpass belief into knowing.

Let us use the analogy of a trip, if I wanted to go to Florida for a vacation from Canada it would take me approximately 3 days to drive there. If I choose to take a plane my traveling time would be shorter, instead of 3 days to arrive it would take me 3 hours. If I could take a sonic jet I would lessen my time significantly, I could be there in a half hour. So traveling on a sonic jet would get me there faster but then I would miss much more in comparisons to the other ways of transportation.

In driving I would experience many more things along the way then I would in the plane or the sonic jet. So which way is actually the best? Any of the choices as it is dependant uniquely on the individual's preferences of what we desired to experience along the way, And also in the choice of traveling time in conjunction with our individual schedules and so on. What will make all the difference is dependent if we desired to see and experiences different sites along the way or not. This can be perceived similar to the contrast we experience in our lives of what we don't want compared to what we do want.

When we compare this to manifesting it can be perceived in the same way. Some of us may take longer or shorter to manifest our desires, again it is all unique because individually we learn and experience different things along the way. So it is not that one way is better then another it is just different experiences along the way dependent upon the person taking the trip. Just as it is dependant on our own selves on how we choose to manifest. The more aware we are will be the more we can consciously with deliberate intention steer our thoughts into the flow of what we want,

It's also important to realize that we can change our minds along the way. If we desired to speed it up we can choose to only keep our most dominant thoughts and feelings on what we desire in harmony. Keep them pure and never altered from trust and knowing they are so close and on their way. That way we get the momentum of vibration to speed up, like a sonic jet. Just like the trip analogy, we could be half way to Florida and decide to change our mind and order a sonic jet or plane from the half way point and zoom there more quickly. So there is no going back in that sense just changing the momentum of the desires to speed up or slow down. We would not need to go back to Canada and start all over again, just because half way through our traveling we decided to make no more pit stops along the way.

We can use the Super Human already evolved individuals as role models (as I wrote about in another chapter) to practice so that we can realize that becoming like the Bewitch family may be closer then we think. To instantly be able to teleport, be aware of telepathy and use it, remote view, and use telekinesis, all the same things that is used in the Bewitch family and the Super Human Individuals. And any individual who is evolving to do more then the normal are doing.

So we are evolving like the Bewitched family and eventually collective consciousness on our planet will catch up and our world will then evolve to be what we were always meant to become.

CRAFT 7

++++++++++++

THE MAGIC LAND OF
CREATIVE FLOWING FUN

We have all experienced and know that when we are having fun time goes by so fast that we are stunned with surprise when we look at the clock. And when we are doing something we are not enjoying the time seems to go so slowly that we dread looking at the clock because the time is going so slow. For starters that shows us that man made time is not the real time.

Then what is real time?

There is no real time. What we refer to as real time is no time, it is just fluid and simultaneously all going on at once, we just don't perceive it that way because we perceive it in slowed down linear perceptions of time in infinite space.

There's lots of spookiness when we delve further into observing Samantha the way she can transport everything and anything out of thin air. Whether it be by the wiggle of her nose or casting a spell or just waving her arms and there's the manifestation of her desire done. Can we pull a rabbit out of a hat for real? Not as magicians do to trick our minds but for real? Could we pull a $100.00 bill out of our wallet if there was no money in it previously? Without any other physical being putting it in either?

There are individuals doing it right now on our planet and we can only really refer to them as being like the Bewitched family. Would you not find that to be a fun and creative thing to do and experience? I am sure most of you would agree that that would be fun and very creative and much of the majority of our planet think that its not possible because of their limiting belief systems.

To the individuals who are doing it they already know that it is possible because they are doing it, experiencing it. They have opened their belief systems to unlimited potentials and are the role models for us to follow.

If you are a skeptical non believer like Abner, you always have the opportunity to travel and see it for yourself of others doing these amazing things. Or searching Sai Baba on the internet and also many of the Super Psychic Children that are scattered throughout the world presently.

Though I have mentioned this in my other books, it's important to all skeptics to search it out if they dare. The book by the authors, Paul Dong and Thomas E. Raffill titled "China's Super Psychics" and more and more children and adults are popping up everywhere around the world. What is also interesting is that when these psychic kids and some adults show other ordinary individuals how to do these things, they learn so easily and then can do the seeming impossible things too. It was also discovered that their DNA is not the same DNA that the normal human body.

As we start to practice these extra ordinary experiences our brain rewires new connections and of course that would change our DNA and activate ones that have been not activated as yet. What science in the past referred to as junk DNA? The only reason science and researchers or scientist referred to it as junk because they did not have any comprehension of what it could be used for, so that was their perception of it. Now we know what junk DNA is for to evolve into becoming bewitching or super human as the Super Human Individuals are showing us.

Now anyone can go to any of these locations to watch these individuals that use amazing abilities and there are seminars going on that they do attend to show us what they can do. Drunvalo Melchizedek has researched and brought this information to the public and some of it can be viewed on you tube. So this is not just theory, this is not just future things that can be done. These are not things that are just reserved for Samantha's family in Bewitched, these are things that are being done by these individuals right now.

Of course the most amazing thing is that if we can practice to do these things for your own self and that is the greatest proven evidence that can ever be. These types of mind expanding practices of doing the extra ordinary things are also fun and creative and it is taking the guidance from higher infinite source. Instead of from just the limited rational mind that has kept humanity stuck for way too long.

So it is dependant on what each individual describes to be fun and creative for themselves. What is fun and creative for one individual may not be for another, we all have our own unique flavoring of what we refer to as fun. And we all experience that when we have are having fun, enjoying what we are doing, creativity seems to magical flow with it. Time becomes so fluid that it becomes almost timeless until we look at the clock and what seemed like five minutes became four or six hours that passed. Then we know we were in the magical space time of space that's referred to timelessness.

Do you also notice that when you are in that magical no time that whatever you are doing seems to have a magical blend of creativeness? Whatever you are doing just seems to be more enlightened and turns out to be more sparked of genius in the way you are thinking or resolving or creating in whatever it is you are doing? We then can realize to know that it's our real natural infinite self or source coming through removed of our rational ego mind interfering. It is sparks showing us what we are to eventually evolve to become, either in our future or now if we take the steps to do what we love to do. That is taking our fun, creative time and selves and expanding it into our daily lives to experience most of our time in that magical way. What a difference that makes in our lives when we can be in that magical fun creative state all day long and get paid for it too. This is where we are headed for collectively, we will all follow that path by the role modeling that others are paving the way for everyone to become to live.

So witches and warlocks of the bewitching life are not reserved for a few, they are our future destinations of what we are going to become and these super role models are showing us how and what they can do for us to eventually become.

If you are not familiar with these super extraordinary bewitching super human individuals, I will share some of their abilities. There powers are so magically bewitching that it takes reading about this a few times to really comprehend the reality of what they can do.

I will refer to them as Star Individuals. Apparently in 1974 there were over 100,000 children then, so the numbers of them now must be astronomical.

One star girl performed her magic to over one thousand people in the audience and each person in the audience was given a live tightly bud rose to hold in their hands. The star girl with her intention and energy bloomed each rose to full bloom within seconds. All of the star children can do it.

Another amazing ability these star individuals can do is while they are blindfolded they can read anything, a book, magazine, paper with their feet, hands, ears and armpits. To add to the amazement they can read anything even when the paper is crumbled and squashed into a ball, with 100% accuracy, being right on. It does not matter if a book was taken from a stack of hundreds of random books and anyone who picks one book and opens it to any page, these star children can read it word for word.

The star children can take a photograph that anyone hands them and still blindfolded explain what and who is on the photo and then expand into the individuals in the photo and what went on in their past and present and possible future too.

Star children can heal at a distance immediately upon their intentions and they never get sick, they are incapable of sickness and are perpetually healthy. Their body cells are already in natural harmony.

Star individuals can teleport objects from one location to another distant location instantly, without any gaps in time or space. They can also pop objects into manifestation from their intentions just like that from seemingly thin air, it just pops in and is there in physical.

Darrin would finally have to give up his nonsense of no longer accepting all this witchery and magic because eventually he will have to go with the evolving flow. So we must ask ourselves the question, are we like Darrin the stubborn doubting rational mind or are we opening up like the rest of the Bewitched family to finally claim and own our magical capabilities to use as these Star Individuals are doing?

These Star Individuals can have a tightly closed vitamin bottle sitting on the table and pop those vitamins out of the bottle and on to the table, the bottle is still securely tightly closed through the whole process. It is just automatic that they know everything is energy and they work with the energy or they know that we are living in a dream and the dream is only as real as we make it. In science we have neutrino's which are properties that can go through any physical object. But whatever the star individuals know, they just do all of these things so easy and effortlessly.. Telepathy is so natural, so you could never keep a secret or lie because they can tune into your thoughts.

Metal bending of course is kindergarten stuff for star individuals, they can do it with one moment of intention bend anything with their minds.

In the 1970's Uri Geller demonstrated his psychic abilities on TV, not only did he bend metal in front of everyone watching but the television audiences experienced the metal at their own homes while observing the show, their metal bent too. The station that televised the show reported floods of calls that came in of what they also were able to do from just observing Uri do it. This is what is referred to the "One Hundred Monkey Effect" if you are not familiar with what it there was a book written about it. One monkey had washed a potato in the lake's water and then it was observed that other monkey from all over the world were doing the same thing.

Let's ponder the ability to be like a neutrino but to be a physical neutrino we become like the bewitching family that always walks through the walls to enter the house. Though we would surely be like Aunt Clara when most of the time she is never able to do it the first time. She tells herself to concentrate and then usually she easily walks through the wall, even though sometimes she lands up in the closet or fireplace. For any limiting skeptical beliefs it will take lots of practice to master this one to be able to walk through walls as the rest of the bewitching family.

Amazingly there are star children that can walk through walls. It was portrayed that the government was playing with this in practices years ago as is revealed in the comedy movie titled, "Men who stare at goats" which is based on all true information that can be viewed in the movie's special features. And many of the government employees who were involved. Remember if one person can walk through walls then we all have the capability to also do it if we desired to.

So really do we want to stay to be like Darrin or Gladys who just watches with amazement or be like Samantha and her family?

Well believe it or not, that is where we heading eventually collectively that will become our reality in our future. These star children and adults are paving the way for us to follow, when we dare to dream the dream and live it.

Imagine Elizabeth Montgomery being alive today? Or maybe she is reincarnated as one of these Star Individuals who are paving the way? I mean we can still only wonder when she passed on from this reality that she might have choose to come back to expand on her journey. But this time without a disguise as in a fictional series but in real physical experiences. Would you not do the same when that is all possible to do and experience in physical, think about it?

These Star Individuals who are really unified, all united in all that they do, they are peaceful healers, showing the world that they have come here for a very needed purpose, to transform the world to peace and paradise and what is many times referred to as heaven on earth.

This is incredible because so much of what Samantha and her family could do these Star Ones are doing. I do not know if they could create a whole room to be filled with furniture if it was not? Or manifest a big hummer out of thin air? However if they can manifest small objects, bigger objects is in for the future magic to become to do. We are going through and on our way to a powerfully magical future of evolving into, it is so bewitching. All seeming impossible will be possible and expanding even from that magnitude and the possibilities are infinite.

So mirror mirror upon the wall, who are the finest of them all? All of us unified to knowing our connection with everything will empower us into our new magical powerful world. We always were deserving of as our creator's rite. Let's brew that into our quantum soup of flavoring to finally taste the magic we all have within us.

CRAFT 8

+++++++++++++

MORE SPOOKY STUFF

INFINITE
DIMENSIONAL
REALITIES

Are you ready to expand your mind more?

To conjure up a brew of more "spooky action at a distance" quoted as Einstein had once said in reference to quantum physics and bring it closer in for an expanded view?

It is when we allow ourselves to go the distance and expand our minds into what may be a bit spooky and even creates the feeling of fear. If we can just let go of some of that fear and become more comfortable with the nature of reality by getting to know what we really are so it can bring us into some seemingly magic brewing.

Let us ponder how the physical personality most refer to as the ego will keep trying to hold on to limited beliefs that perpetually convince us that we are just solid beings and everything around us is solid too. Even though old classical science has shown us that under powerful microscopes that everything that appears solid is moving atom of particles. Then as science expanded to show us that those moving particles can also transform into wave properties too.

It's through our senses of sight, smell, touch, hearing and tasting that we use to perceive our objective world. Even though it is common knowledge and believed that this is all true yet we live our daily lives without the awareness and take so much for granted.

Just as a actor plays a part of character in a movie and then after the filming the actor goes back to their own personality self.

So that non physical feeling of experience, that dreamily feeling we get as a result, and if it is not physical then it also could be referred to as a dream. The state we are in while experiencing it is dreamily, you must admit? It is the dream within a dream, it is the physical you letting go of your physical dream for the moments of the non physical dream.

Let us expand more into what a dream really is. When you fall asleep and awaken from a dream that you so vividly remember and if you really delve into all the specifics you can admit that it felt so real. You awoke in a sweat from running, you even felt blush if you were running in the nude. You recall the colors and feelings as if it was so real, so then you know that it was real but your limited mind says no it was just a dream. Think about this, if you never awoke from that dream, where would you be? You would be living in another reality that you would forget about this one because all your focus now is in that one. To the limited mind it may even be a little scary to even think about, however one day when the mind expands to be more comfortable with this idea it will actually be consciously expanding of the joy that expanded consciousness brings.

To describe infinite to unlimited minds is a challenge until the comfort level is expanded enough to comprehend it, because of the solidness that our senses gives us. When we break everything down to an energy wave like state is when infinite can have more of a grasp to understand, and is where all possibilities are.

So when we are in a dream the reason it feels so real when you awake is because it was real while you were giving 100% focus into it. When you awoke your attention of focus came back to this reality, which is another focus of your attention. So what are dreams really, and what are intense imaginings or day dreaming? The same thing, just different focuses of attention. And what are all these different focuses of attention for? For the experiences to experience in different realities, different dreams, different characters, infinite of varieties. Could also be the reason that movies, soap operas and fictional stories are and have always been so popular? Everything that our external reality shows us is just a sparking of what the infinite reality is.

CRAFT 9

++++++++++++

STIRRING THE QUANTUM SOUP

How fantastically magical it was when quantum physics showed in experiments that the one observing the experiments actually affected the results of the experiments. That stirring of the quantum soup of experiments they found evidence that things in our reality are not what they thought or expected it to be. It is much more magical, much more seeming mysterious then we have all been taught in the old science. Even though ancient wisdom and masters of the ancient wisdom always knew it.

We are coming to realize that the real genie is the observer all intertwined, as the observer does effect the observed, it is the creating process entangled and working together. Affecting everything in it's path. Instead of the myth of three wishes from the genie, the wishes are really infinite, eternally, and is perpetually going on minutely.

As for many of us who have studied to learn and experimented before quantum physics started showing all this magical brewing before it was reported to the media and public. Many of us have already been doing our own experiments. Getting our guidance from many of the out of the ordinary channels of guides and many were not even physical beings. They were from humans channeling the information that quantum physics became to prove. Or was it that a collective bunch of us subconsciously created the quantum evidence so that it would be brought out into the mainstream and for the public to know.

What quantum physics allowed was for all superstition to be laid to rest once and for all. Those old beliefs were only leverage for a time because many believed if they could not understand something, if it was out of the comprehension it was referred to as a label of superstition. We also know that all the dogma in religions did seem to add into the concoctions that stirred up the superstition too.

Presently it really does not matter, all that matters is that by our own experiences we experience the quantum magic in our own lives. That is where the proof really matters and takes a powerful stand. When we can wave our magical wands, being our imagination to focus with feeling on what we desire is already ours and received our manifestation, is really connecting the dots for us. We come to realize that as we observed what we wanted long enough with absolute certainty, feeling as if it is already in our possession, it becomes into our experience.

What we did was observe a desire and that constant observation changed the outcome to be what it is. If we observed with doubt and lack that is what we get, if we observe with trust and expectation, that is what we get, what we wanted. It becomes quite simple after practicing it with the repetition needed and every individual will have their own time lapse. The time lapse in the manifestation is only dependant on each individual that is creating dependant on what their beliefs consist of.

Each one of us personally creates the gap or lapse in time for our desired manifestations to be received. If there is allot of doubt then the time lapse may take a long time because that doubt has to transform to trust. The lapsing gap of in between times of chosen desire has to be structured. We structure it by thinking about the desire until that desire moves from doubt, to maybe its possible. Then to more feelings of possibilities, then it moves to yes we feel it's a probability, to yes it can happen, to it will happen. When we get into the stronger later structuring of the desire by seeing and feeling as if it is already ours as if we received it, that generates the fuel to solidify all those quantum waves of possibilities into becoming received in physical reality. That is what is meant by the observer effect, we observe long enough with an expectation of what we get.

This is quite similar to Darrin always waiting for whoever has cast the spell on him to reverse the spell so he can experience what he wants. He always desires to be back to his normal self however does not realize that he has the power within himself to not allow the spells to affect him. Darrin's beliefs are so strong that he is always believing that others can affect him by their hypnotic spells. If he were to take his power back, his timing of his desire to no longer be under others spells would not only have less waiting time to be back to normal, he'd never be under the disempowering influence to begin with. Just as conditioning does for us.

The extremely important thing not miss here is that along the structure of time lapsing we are still always creating. Just as Darrin does with his waiting for the spells to be removed or reversed. Even if we're not creating what we desire or want like Darrin, we are still creating in alignment to what we expect by our beliefs. If we expect in the doubting stages then that is what we are constantly creating and receiving. So creating is continuously going on in exact alignment with what we expect. We may think that we expect our desire but if we feel doubtful about it that is our expectation we receive.

So we can think of it as a huge witches brew of quantum soup. The soup sits there as infinite possibilities until we start to stir the soup by focusing in on a desire. The more we focus on the desire as if it is already owned and received, we are like heating or baking it up to create it to be received in physical. But you don't want to over cook the brewing soup because if you do you will spoil the flavor, just as if you add any doubt then you have over boiled and delayed the results. So it is important to let it simmer and every time we think of our desire do so with complete trustful knowing it is on its way. Letting go is similar to turning the brewing soup burner off and letting it cool down a bit, you'll know it is ready.

Do you doubt when you can see and feel the soup as your mind thinking, feeling and seeing it as real? No, you just trust it is brewing and now brewed and soon you will be tasting the soup, which will be your manifested desire received. Just as we would not keep going to the stove and checking the pot to make sure the brew is still in the pot. No we just know because we put all the ingredients in the pot, so we trust it is still there not disappeared. That is the trusting part, we let go, that's the cooking time and then walla and it is done.

The pot was neutral until we observed the empty pot, just as the quantum soup of all possibilities, just as all possibilities are neutral until we choose one. We then gathered and added all we wanted into the pot which is our specifics of our desires and then brewed it until it was cooked. Just as whenever the thought of our desire

77

pops up throughout the day is like stirring the soup. We let it simmer which is like trusting and letting go knowing it's on its way, it will be cooked to perfection. Then it manifests and we enjoy our brew, our desire created to us in physical.

When we do this with enough repetition we become to know that this is how creating reality works and we keep experimenting until we get it perfected from practicing. Then we look into the mirror and instead of asking what we are and what are we capable of, we then know. Then we pronounce with such knowing certainty and exclaim from our hearts, I know I am a creator creating. I really do see that it was always me creating, even when I was not aware of what I was doing, now I now know!

CRAFT 10

+++++++++++++

BREAKING OUT OF
CONDITIONED SPELLS

Since we now know that there are other individuals doing what seems to be bewitching on our planet that allows it to be easier for us to become the magical miraculous beings we are capable of being. They have broken the limits of what seemed impossible to know that so much more is now possible if we dare to go into the unknown to experience it for our own selves.

Others have broken out of the hypnotic spell of limited seeming logical conditioning that has kept most believing in limitations and seemingly impossible. So that our lives in physical can become just like in Bewitched, to finally let go of all the old limiting beliefs that dictated us to be enslaved to anything we do not enjoy. That our lives then can become purely joyful in everything we do, to be able to finally take the easy path of not only least resistance, but of no resistance. Wouldn't it make more sense that our lives should become effortless and magical the way it may have been destined to evolve to become?

Once and for all we become to absolutely know that we are no longer going to associate and be like Abner because that is the old ways that limit our capabilities. The old way of thinking is that if these amazing abilities are impossible and the only way to justify it as being done through a scam or trickery of some sort. That is the hypnotic rational beliefs that keep most spinning in a web of limits and staying in the same old box, old thinking. If we are going to choose to become more like the Bewitched family and learn to use more and more of our powers as we expand.

So how do we do it? How do we become like the Bewitch family?

In the old way we still believe that we must practice and practice until we master to perfect what we desire to do. Yet once an individual breaks original limits then others follow. Just as many are doing with spoon bending, first with physical touching then without physical touching and just with our powerful energy as in telekinesis.

There is an easier way and a faster way which would be to connect to another reality another dimensional self that has already mastered it and can help us do it more instantly. If many of the old beliefs are now dropped and newer powerful expanded wisdom has been developed then it will be easy to connect and then just do what we intend to do. That eliminates all the practicing time because we are trying to just do it without the help of other selves or entities that are always available to help us when we ask and tap or tune in. When we choose to do it the easier available way, then we allow an open connection in the asking of a desire that allows that help to come to us. As Burt Goldman teaches which he calls "quantum jumping", which is the wisdom of the knowing there are infinite realities going on simultaneously. When we open up to them then we allow the already desired energy to come through us, which we then can sit down at a piano and just play beautiful melodies as Nicole Whitney. Or as Burt Goldman paints beautiful paintings. Either way will get us to our desire, one is just faster and easier, the other way of practicing is longer.

Are We Predicting Reality or Creating It?

For myself I pondered to go deeper under the veil of what may appear as illusions we have been hypnotized to believe in, to understand what we are actually doing with seeing through cards or anything when we are creating. We already have become to know that the power is in the present moment, which breaks us free from the hypnotic state of linear time and beliefs. Which then allows us to comprehend to understanding that everything is occurring simultaneously, all at the same time. Once we truly grasp with comprehending that truth, then it makes it easier for us to go deeper to ponder predictions versus creating. Are we really predicting to see the unrevealed card before we physically see it, or are we creating it before we see it? That is a powerful question to ponder because that also makes a big difference in how we are believing our reality does work. The old way under the hypnotic suggestions that influence us to believe that everything is a steady continuum that would then allow us to accurately predict reality. The new way which is breaking through that illusion, which is also breaking out of the old conditioned hypnotic trance then states we are creating by the moment. This makes a profound difference then in everything in our lives, in our reality and gives us such a powerful way to use our reality.

Like an imprinted residue burned into my memory I can hear Bashar's voice of spoken words explaining, how that is not the same quarter in my hand, that's a different quarter. In reference when

Bashar, channeled by Darryl Anka asked the audience to take any object into one of their hands, and some individuals took a quarter. Then he asked the audience to move that quarter or object to the other hand and then went on to explain that is not the same object or quarter, it is a different quarter or object. It only appears as the same object because of our beliefs that direct our perceptions of continuity making it appear as if it is the same object from one hand to the other, but in true reality it is not. All the variables and properties instantaneously change, just like that.

Now, I remind you, you are reading my book of the evolving reality of Bewitched, which is the evolving reality of where we are heading, so don't expect mortal talk? Of course not, we are really delving into the good brew of stuff, to go where the power and truth of reality is, not the illusions. You are free to take whatever resonates with you and leave the rest, eventually if we are to evolve past illusions to the real truth of reality then we must expand ourselves further. To become bewitched we must expand our minds into what seems to be the unknown to know and this is the journey we are becoming to evolve upon. So if it seems a bit spooky at first it will take some mind bending then to expand into it. We have chosen to no longer stay and be little baby creators we have chosen to become more masterful creators, adult creators with knowledge that turns into our wisdom, we are growing spiritual beings into our physical beings. So we must expand our limiting beliefs to go the distance to know the real truths, yes just like our babyish beliefs in santa to become to know that there is no real santa in the north pole. To even go beyond into the knowledge that we really are the santa's, we really are the bewitches, we really are creators creating reality. For us who dare to go further into the unknown to know we let go of the illusions that being in a hypnotic state of the old limited reality to know what the new reality is expanding to become.

Remember we have now made the choice to no longer be like Darrin and become like Samantha and her bewitching family and the more we stretch ourselves to know makes all the difference. It is accepting our divine heritage and powerful abilities. The more we use our powers the more perfected they also become, just as when Samantha's home became like a vapor energy that no one could leave the home after they arrived. It was because Samantha choose to not use her powers as she did in her past before meeting Darrin that created the being stuck. She had to keep using her powers to unlock the vapor of vibration that kept everyone stuck, just as we become stuck in our old ways. The new powerful ways unlock us from the hypnotic illusion of what is possible and what we may think is not, when everything is possible when we choose to know it.

So could this be the hypnotic spell we really are under?

A spell of social conditioning that we gave our powers away to everything other then our own self. Believing and trusting in the authorities as government, doctors, teachers, media and so on of the limited old ways, old beliefs, any disempowering ways, instead of trusting and knowing our natural powerful true selves where all the wisdom and power resides. Taking the guidance from the limited conditions that tell us what we should do and think and believe in the hypnotic spell of the limited beliefs of being victims that need to be dictated to. Instead of guiding us as the most masterful wise teachers do for those who are open to take the guidance of returning ourselves to ourselves. Owning our power and expanding our consciousness to then be able to live a heavenly life on earth.

Many times as we watch the Bewitched show all Samantha has to do is snap her fingers and the spell is broken. Darrin then thinks he is free, however he really never is because any other member of the bewitched family can create another spell on him, so he is never really free, that is an illusion. The only way Darrin could be free would be if he were to learn the power and become a powerful being himself, then he would no longer be instantly hypnotized under their spells. His freedom would lie in himself, but he is so conformed to the limiting reality that he is stuck to always be controlled by the bewitched family, just as we are if we let ourselves be controlled by authority.

Darrin would need to unite with them, learn from them and go beyond his limited reality to join in with them instead of perpetually resisting their reality. They are all in a reality yet Darrin is in his limited stuck reality and the Bewitched family are in they're unlimited reality and not stuck or controlled. We can then realize that they are all in a physical reality with different realities going on dependent upon their perceptions and beliefs.

Now which reality would you prefer to be in, Darrin's or the bewitched family? And I am quite certain that if everyone knew it was a real possibility to have all the powers then most would choose Bewitched ways. The only thing stopping anyone is the belief that continues to dictate that is not possible. When we continue to practice and do what was only seems not possible to experience ourselves doing the possible, then we cannot deny our power. We have proven it to our own selves and nothing or no one can alter us from that knowledge of wisdom, it is our absolute knowing, our truths. Then we have joined the bewitched family and are role models for all the Darrin's in the world.

So breaking the hypnotic spell that keeps us bound in illusions is breaking the limiting beliefs of the conformed reality that is controlling the majority with suggestions that they choose to suggest to us. Instead of us choosing our own more potential suggestions that will break us free from their limiting suggestions. Once we break through that spell of conditioning we become so free and magical and own our own selves and we become to know that all is really possible. How magnificently bewitching is that?

CRAFT 11

+++++++++++++

HALLOWEEN & CHRISTMAS SIMILARITIES

Halloween and Christmas are so in tune and have many similarities to show us they're deeper meanings that can expand our wisdom to even join them together into **Christoween**. We could create a new holiday that combines the two into **Christoween** and celebrate it in the middle of the calendar year which is the month of June and have it on the 13th which is half way through the month. So let's say **Christoween** is on June 13th in celebration of the wisdom and evolving of the merged of Halloween with Christmas to really give it zapping power to expand more evolving vibration.

To take the merging of the two **Christoween** back to separateness we will define the two holidays of Christmas and Halloween of their similarities.

Halloween is filled with magic, power, dressing up to be something we are not, like an actor be a part of movie. We can trick or we can treat, knowing that all tricks have the treats within because there is always knowledge behind a trick. All tricks give an illusion to make them appear as real. Just as our reality is, appearing as a trick to the rational mind of old ways of thinking but when we unveil the secretive truth behind the illusions of the trick we can then see the nature of reality. The truth that reveals how the trick is played out but behind the trick is the way it really functions to make it appear as a trick.

Christmas is similar to Halloween as it is a magical time we celebrate the birthday of a man, the son of god, our sibling who could do the same kinds of things as Samantha in Bewitched. He could turn water into wine, heal the sick, feed thousands by expanding a few loaves of bread into many. So Christ we could say did the same things as Samantha could do, they were both magical and left us with mystery to unfold.

Magical Miracles

Christ was a master of reality and Samantha was a witch a master of her reality, they were doing the same things, the only differences were their labels given. Christ was a master who could create miracles, witch masters could create through spells, When we remove all labeling and judgments and just perceive them unveiled we can know they are doing the same things. So we created to keep witches with Halloween and Christ with religion and then there was everything else in between. Quantum physics is merging them, so instead of separating all the referrals and labeling, we instead see it all as one, to combine magic and miracle as one, a magical miracle. Magic and miracles is really the same thing with only minute variations through description, one leaning with religion in a divine flavoring the other with mystic of an occult flavoring, yet doing the same things.

It is important to realize that one seems spookier and the other seems just as spooky depending on the observer and what the observer defines as spooky. What we believe is the key factor.

What is the difference if a witch turned water into win compared to Christ? They are both doing the same thing, manipulating reality, transforming molecules, atom, or particles into wave properties with their inspirational intentions and desires.

Christians believe that Christ is the spirit that comes through for miracles and a witch creates magic through spells and incantations as the Bewitching family did. Both Christ and witches were punished by others who feared their powers, Christ was crucified and witches were beheaded and burned. This seemed to create a consciousness to keep the majority of the population in fear so that they could be controlled by the ones who created those limiting beliefs originally to be in control.

So if we are doing extraordinary things like a Witch or Christ then we are really the same with just a different label. Christ was also a human just connected consciously with his Infinite Creator that allowed him his power. A witch is the same connected to her heritage that allows the flow of her power. Both are human and experiencing what appears to have been conditioned to dictate these powers as non accepted in human or mortal form. Whoever was doing the dictating or controlling in past history and labeling to define the meanings spiced with what type of beliefs? It was rational altered personality's that were in fear and could not expand into more of what we really are, our powerful heritage to come to own.

Old unlimited beliefs are thoughts that were valued too long and became stagnant which is being unwilling to change, when we know change is inevitable and what reality naturally does. Change is to expand and evolve into more then we were in the past, to become more and when we become more we become more powerful too. More is to expand in more knowledge that allows us to become of more wisdom through our own experiences. Not worship a Christ or Witch, but become as they are, use them as our role modeling to expand ourselves into, which I believe was their intention originally.

In religion prayers are used, with witches spells or incantations are used, what really is the difference? They are both words formed and said to bring about a result. So the in between of Christmas and Halloween we could use meditation to combine prayer and spells. Since prayers, spells, incantations, affirmations and meditation are only tools to get us to that same gap or zone of the infinite source of all that is, where all the power is. Does it really matter then which tool we use? Since all these tools will get us to that one state of being anyway. So the tool is not the power, it is the gap or zone of infinite beingness that we get to that is important or our desire. So it does not matter if one is using prayers or using spells or a individual using meditation, it is still one person using something with a label as a tool to get us all into the same source where all the power resides.

Taking all of that into consideration then we must realize that quantum physics is merging everything into one. Just as our reality will eventually evolve to do and this is where merging Halloween and Christmas together as one would be a new revised merging of two holidays that are similar in their constructs to one. One powerful day that can expand backwards in perception from June to January, while simultaneously going forward from June to December. While simultaneously effecting all the months from one powerful point of wise knowledge as **Christoween** would do. It is a condition with old potential variables mixed together to give more power and esteem in a celebration to enjoy our empowerment. **Christ** for the vibration of Christmas with the miracle affect and the **oween** of the magical affect into mass as a whole collectively to becoming. To ween ourselves not away but ween ourselves into this empowering state of being, with the 'we' in the ween as WE collectively in consciousness expand to accept our power. I think that would be a very empowering holiday to celebrate.

On **Christoween** we can choose to do whatever we want to do, be it give gifts or candy and dress up and have a celebration of sharing new ideas and new powers we have experienced through using with others we love. Then the rest of the months of the year becomes different because we know that **Christoween** is approaching. So instead of trying to pick gifts for others as we do for Christmas or what candy to give out, we instead use the other months to develop and expand our creative ideas. Which we practice or expand to succeed at extraordinary experiences and then share them with others on that celebrated day.

So throughout the year we are constantly not only empowering ourselves, we are using our creativity of our infinite source to do it which always creates extraordinary things and experiences. Becoming god like as the creators we are destined to become in physical, removed from the drudgery of each day being the same, instead our days become magical and extraordinary daily. Simultaneously it also keeps us in the flow of bliss, ecstasy, fun, excitement, joy, genius, magical, empowered, adventurous expanding creators of creation. Which simultaneously keeps us healthy, wise and aligned with our desires that continuously manifest, it is a most beneficial way of flowing in our lives. This type of holiday would evolve us to expand throughout the year and in alignment with perpetual expanding experiences. If the collective consciousness of our planet eventually followed it all we would also have changed our reality and ripple effect of the whole.

All the spookiness would melt away as in every trick the treat of knowing is already rectified and expanded into the knowledge to be wise to. All labels are dropped so we no longer separate our perception of a Christ or a witch, or a spiritual person, we become seen as one combined, of a **Christoween.**

It may sound a bit outrageously uncomfortable to even consider these new changes, yet from a deeper level you may resonate with some validity in it. The rational mind will try to knock it down, get back to reality but our real infinite self knows it is a great exuberant idea and is comfortable with it. That part of us knows that it is the way to grow and evolve from our drudgery of day to day life with no sparks left. It is time for new ideas of creativity to sustain our evolving momentum, so that we can live each day with the spark of our Infinite Source of all that is, the Creator that holds it all together.

CRAFT 12

+++++++++++++

ARE WE CREATING
OR
PREDICTING REALITY?

When we watch or observe Samantha and her bewitching family we know with out any doubt the answer that they are creating in the moment so instantaneously. Whenever any of Samantha's family puts a spell on Darrin they also can predict in close proximity to the outcome, not of absolute certainty, but quite close. The whole reason that Endora puts the spells on Darrin is because she can see the flow of probability of how Darrin is going to act just from her intention, so they become co-creator's in a sense. Endora is predicting that Darrin is going to mess his reality up however through it learn some exuberant lessons, which is similar to what we are all doing ourselves.

Most of us went through many challenges and became to realize that all we have to do is observe our present reality to know what our beliefs and focused thought has already created for us. It is then that we can realize that if our reality has experiences we do not want, then it is up to ourselves to change it by changing what we focus on most of the time during our day. We can be a Darrin but instead of always being under Endora's spells we can finally break free to own our selves so that our future can become what we do want, of our own control.

Breaking free from the old conditions we have believed in that no longer resonate with what we do not want into new beliefs we do want to see manifest. By knowing that we can break free from the old hypnotized spells of old conditioning, it does not matter how the old beliefs even came about that we have followed until now. The most important thing is to realize that these old beliefs is what created our reality up until now. Our power lies in this present now and how we choose to focus and attach our thoughts too now that will expand into the new creations of our future to become what we do want.

This allows ourselves to become free from any old enslavements that dictated our creation and become our own powerful selves, aware by constantly observing what we are thoughts we are choosing too. It is those thoughts that we consciously choose that expands as we verbally speak the words that are aligned with those thoughts. We always have the power to choose and become creators with deliberate awareness of what we are creating by being aware and this is what gives us our power back.

Then we can realize through awareness and focus of how our future is going to manifest into through the unfolding daily. We will be able to predict the momentum of change as we continue to be aware and pick thoughts that are going to makes us feel more blissful and in aligned with creating what we do want. Even though we can get a larger view and feel for how our future path will change with it's unfolding, we cannot absolutely know every specific prediction. Just as Endora with Darrin, she just knows he will learn from the challenges but he will mess things up along the way. So he will be creating chaos first and after the spell is taken off he then can know what he learned from the experience. That learning then creates the chaos to become structured again into an organized unfolding into his expanding future reality, like a ripple or domino effect. Just as we are doing when we become aware of what we are thinking most of the time because those thoughts then create the emotions and the two forces together create our reality.

It is for the very reason that we all have free will that allows us to realize that in any moment we can then change the direction our life to how it will unfold to become.

This is where it gets a bit foggy and where we may question if we are predicting our future or creating it because our outcome is still foggy. If we think good feeling optimistic thoughts most of the day then we can almost predict that the next few weeks are going align us with more good things to feel good about. But if we think some good thoughts and then think some not good thoughts then we are mixing our brewing of our reality with allot of contrasting flavoring. So our future is going to unfold in the creation of a roller coaster ride with a mixture of experiences which some will feel good and some may feel not as good. Now if we had more focus on the not so feeling good thoughts more then anything, then our future will become in the experiences of what then appears of lots of disappointments and things we probably did not want. We still created that reality to unfold into those manifestations because we gave more attention to lower vibration thoughts.

As an example lets observe that Darrin just found out he was under one of Endora's spells and whether he's aware or not that he was do the choosing, we are always choosing. So he chooses an old automatic response of anger, he becomes angry and speaks some negative words to Endora. Well we can all predict the outcome is going to be Endora becomes revengeful back. So she then casts another spell on Darrin. So he reacted with a lower vibration of anger which is surely affecting his future momentum of enfolding reality. Now if he were to respond in a higher vibration of love and instead respond to Endora with telling her yes he has learned a lesson from these challenges, maybe he learned to be more compassionate to Samantha. So he forgives Endora then she feels better and he feels better and Samantha feels better, it is a beneficial situation of experiences. Those beneficial thoughts that become feelings are higher vibrations and then are expanding in the unfolding of the future with a momentum of even better experiences to unfold and be created. As we observe we can get a clearer perception of the differences of how the future is becoming, so Darrin's reaction or responding is going to effect the outcome. So even if we were to predict the outcome of Darrin's reactions, that outcome we predicted has the flexibility embedded in it if Darrin changes his attitude and responds differently. Then the prediction is false because we always have free will.

It is the free will that we have that allows us to change in any moment. We could choose to stay in anger for a few days or for a few moments which makes all the difference in how the ripple effect will be created to be and effect the unfolding future of experiences. So it does seem that we are always creating reality and the very reason many predictions can be wrong.

So the question do we predict our reality or create our reality? We are really creating our reality by the moment and the moment is continuously unfolding. It is in every moment that we are so powerful that we are constantly affecting our own future. When we start to really go beyond peaking into reality and desire to know how it is being creating by the moments that then shows us how the continuity becomes to unfold into our manifesting created reality. When we are not aware of what we are doing with our thinking then we our perceiving our life as fragmented separate frames as we would view a slide show. When we become aware we then can see it in the same way if we were to put all the slides together and create it onto a video cassette. Anytime we desire to change any frame of the continuity of the video we also can stop it anywhere along the tape and add in something else or delete something on the video tape. We could compare it to our linear time in how we perceive it and use it throughout each day, either with awareness or not makes all the difference of what will become. Then to ask ourselves do we predict or create our reality? We then can clearly see that we are creating it with each thought as a slide that will effect what we put on the video to watch. Because we can change it at anytime because of our free will, we are always in a creating process, which leaves not much potency to predicting. Unless we continue to react the same way with the same attitudes and beliefs with very little change then we can be very predictable.

This brings me then to wondering and questioning many other experiences in our lives as the lottery and other practiced disciplines or perceiving anything we do throughout our days. In the lottery experience when we are checking our tickets after the draw our rational mind will tell us that the numbers are already drawn, so if our numbers do not match we did not win, but if the numbers matched we won something. However, is we delve a bit deeper into reality giving consideration for predicting or creating reality it takes on a different angle of how it works. When we check our tickets with absolute certainty and expectation that we won, does that change the reality in the moment? If we are that powerful to effect our reality in the moment of observation as quantum physics seems to prove in the experiments it shows that we do. The observing collapses the wave of probabilities into solid particles of physical creation. It is in the moment of observing that actually affects the reality to become what we expect it to.

Now that is not only a powerful realization but also very puzzling indeed because rational linear thinking not only suggests but has told us that when we check our tickets it is dependant on beliefs of random luck. The numbers are drawn and if our numbers match all numbers drawn that we are a winner of a jack pot prize. But quantum physics is showing us that reality does not work that way, it is not dependant on random luck that creates the reality, it is dependant on how we observe the checking of the ticket, or an experiment. If we check the ticket with the expectation from a belief that we are not feeling lucky and did not win then that is just the way it goes. So in quantum states of reality we all in what appeared to be a powerful moment, which is a momentum of vibrational frequencies that have stirred up the waves of possibilities to become reorganized dependant on how we observe our checking the ticket. If we observe it with beliefs that we are never lucky, we will create the outcome to be not lucky, our prediction will become true, the evidence will support itself through the observation. Our expectation will match and collapse our reality to become created to be the evidence of not winning again. If we expect with the belief that we always win small amounts then that expectation will create that outcome to support our evidence. If we expect to win the jackpot with absolute knowing that we really do have that lucky energy or that we are aware that our observance does effect the expect outcome to collapse the wave, we would win.

Have I stirred the brew of wondering and questioning on this subject? When it comes to money and lottery's especially now when the so called recession is upon us and more and more our learning and wondering about the nature of reality. Especially since quantum physics has been showing us all of its weird experiments that is showing us that reality is not what we it seemed to be as in the linear rational minds thinking, the old way. It is revealing much more spooky or weird happenings that is expanding, stretching our consciousness to know more of what is going on and how it is going on. Right in synchronicity of what all the wise ancient masters always knew about reality. Where all the wisdom of knowledge is now merged with science and religions however into now our reality. Not in some heaven we die and go to, but to a heavenly magical existence here on earth.

Back to the questioning of the lottery outcomes in the moment of checking a ticket, are we predicting or creating? In a sense it is both, if we feel lucky or are wise to reality then we are predicting our creation with certainty either way, lucky or not. The evidence is in the outcome, it is only the way an individual observes the expectation to become. So where does luck have to do with any of it? It seems to be that luck is just a label for a vibration that is always in creation of creating, dependant on what we think to feel most of the time, most dominantly. Dominantly as in the domino effect of what will unfold to become on what we expect it to become controlled by what we believe. Then that leads us further down the rabbit hole into how can that possibly be when the numbers are already drawn and the lottery corporation knows the matched winning numbers and even can determine and knows the store the ticket was bought from. The corporation knows the store of the winning ticket and the numbers that were already drawn. The person already claimed they're winning prize, but what if you were to check your ticket and also won the jack pot and matched all the numbers, but they're was no split in the money. Now we must really go into the leading edge here to comprehend the unfolding reality of this.

Are you ready, really ready for the most probable answer?

Okay, here we go, in that moment your reality shifts and that includes your whole being shifts to the realty that this manifestation is occurring and everything follows suit to unfold in whatever way it unfold to be the outcome. Now unless we were on that leading edge with all of our beliefs would also be needed to be able to even create the reality to be comprehended to begin with, which most of us are not so this would not be the creation. Most when hearing that another person already won the jackpot singular with no splitting of the jack pot and because that is the reality we are in coherent with, we would also agree. We would check our ticket and not have won or come close. But if we were on the leading edge with absolute knowing of how reality works like in quantum states, then we would shift and become into another reality where we are the winner in that reality and there is no other. Yes it would instantly just become the outcome and everything would unfold to fit into that reality immediately, past and future all collapsed into one reality of winning the whole jack pot.

I know this is really stretching or expanding our consciousness to even be able to comprehend that the nature of reality works this way. We would then have to be wise to the pondering as many researchers are doing now, that there may be multiple realities or even infinite realities. If we are to use that frame of reference then that would allow our rational minds to try to accept how that would work. Because if there are infinite realities then we could then understand how we could switch anytime to any one of them from our expectations. So then if we shifted to another reality that we won, then not only the corporation has all unfolded to support our expectation and the outcome. I myself have this knowing there are infinite realities and that we are doing the switching instantaneously and all of the time.

It's our habitual automatic senses of perception that gives our reality that continuous momentum that make it always appear as if we are always in the same reality. An illusion of continuation. However if we go to the quantum level of states then we surely become wise to the comprehension of infinite realities and how it is possible that we are constantly shifting. This data also gives us the wisdom in knowing that we also are always creating reality, it is so fluid and ever changing by each moment, which is simultaneously creating the expectations of the outcome. Which is creating the outcome while simultaneously is expanding our consciousness in the evolving states to become even wiser masters at mastering reality. It takes on a whole new dimension of perception then the old limiting way, which we also know that the new evolving way is to expand the old limits into unlimited infinitely.

Does all this expanded knowledge change the way we would perceive to check our tickets? I would think so because we would have to agree if we were to align ourselves with quantum physics. It is what shows us that this is what is occurring in reality even if we are still unable to grasp the understanding with our limited beliefs of awareness, it is what it is showing us as a model for reality. That we are creating reality by the moment, that anything is possible, that nothing stands still for long, it is always changing and expanding and infinitely.

In every moment we are creating reality, moment by moment as it unfolds. Our perception must change from one that perceives to take pieces out of a box of puzzles and putting them together to we no longer have a box of pieces. We are creating the puzzle as we go picking up pieces from everywhere and anywhere, not from the linear finite box. We are picking pieces from a quantum brew that is not even in a pot or box but infinite hologram, which is not contained in any measurement of circumferences, because it is always expanding and cannot be boxed in. We must perceive it with new references that expand and keep expanding. When we try to rationalize it we only loose the focus because it is not rational it is expanding quantum states of reality.

This should leave you with many things to ponder about reality, to expand your consciousness into many infinite dimensional realities, which one, which you? Power seems to go hand in hand with this expansion, of course because we always become what and how we observe. We are creators creating our realities by the moment of the momentum that we are doing it. The bewitched family just takes it naturally as their heritage and does not question they're powers they just use it. Christ took his natural divine heritage too and the powers that went with it.

We are questioning our reality because we desire to become powerful to be able to use the powers. It may be that once we are able to use the powers we no longer question it because it was our questioning that allowed us evolve to using our powers. We then are divinely bewitched and know it and continue to expand into more wise knowledge that can enhance our potentiality of our divine magical selves. Into easy, free, loving, magically miraculous beings we were destined to be in physical embodiment. Then to experience what we could do in the spiritual dimensions so easily and to experience now in the physical, for the exuberant magical experiences we are unfolding into. May magical miraculous bewitching be your enfolding life to keep the brew brewing because the infinite expands more for us to unfold to experience along our ways.

CRAFT 13

++++++++++++

RELEASED OF THE SUPERSTITIOUS SPELL OF THE # 13

In the past the number 13 had superstition attached to it and there still may be some individuals who are living their lives with the belief that 13 is an omen or negative to be still perceived of superstition. Since most of us reading this book have already come to the undeniable conclusion that we create our reality, which means all of our reality. We have become more like the thinking of the Bewitching family which I am sure they either see the power in the number or do not believe there is any significance in it at all.

How can it have any substance to it when we take it to it's neutral state of nothingness. It's the we give it meaning and then that meaning will define what we attach to it and then create our reality as a result It is just a number, however if we go looking for positive or negative about the number 13 we will find it. The same way we will find anything because everything is recorded in the holographic memory banks of the infinite consciousness. So it will always be up to our own self to choose what we want to think about the number 13 or any number. Again it will all depend on our beliefs and everyone always has free will to believe what they want to believe. So there will always be something to justify either way, lucky or unlucky depending on what one believes in.

Thirteen is becoming more of a luckier number then in the past as more individuals are associating luck and positive thoughts about it. They have taken the old meaning and transferred a new empowering meaning to it to make it be more divine or to their advantage. It will always to our advantage to give empowering definitions of meaning to everything because then we know we are then creating in alignment with want we want instead of what we do not want. Most can agree that they would rather be lucky then unlucky, however the hidden beliefs that can dictate our reality is what the culprit is. By changing the definition we change the meaning we give anything and that literally changes the energy which changes our reality and will reflect that new meaning. This gives life a magical blending vibration to everything, it could be perceived as sparkling magic dust on everything. Seeing the beauty and opportunity in everything and not defining it as negative but instead of an opportunity to expand ourselves into the magical miraculous loving state we prefer.

We could use some numerology and take the number 13, unite it by adding the two digits, $1 + 3 = 4$, four is a even number turning the original oddness of 13 to even. In some traditions they may believe the number 4 to be powerful or divine. All dependant on beliefs again. This is the magnificence magic of the ability to creatively attach meaning to define anything in new way.

We realize we can search through humanity's history and find many meanings of the number 13, some things to be lucky and some things to be unlucky. Yet I repeat again, that it will not make any difference to us if we believe that everything is of our most power to bring it back into it's powerful neutral state and then create it to be whatever idea we choose for it to be.

We can take a closer look at some things that presently still have the number thirteen or 13 things in the objects. This gives me the impression that thirteen for whoever has used thirteen had applied a powerful meaning to their definitions. Then we have our own free will to take it from there and believe whatever we want.

CRAFT 14

+++++++++++++

BREWING THE WAVE & PARTICLE PROPERTIES

We can be like Samantha who is always happy and putting any pieces that Darrin perceives as chaotic but for Samantha she knows it all part of the process of change.

For example in the show Bewitched there is something chaotic always going on with Samantha's family always casting spells and intruding in Samantha and Darrin's life. Even though Darrin and Samantha realized they were going to have challenges because of the choices they made with intermingling a relationship with a witch and a mortal.

So taking all of that into consideration we realize that chaos is a daily occurrence with Samantha and Darrin, just as it is with our lives too. When we perceive chaos as challenging situation and become like Samantha, we always add positive thoughts to anything that comes our way. Like Samantha we too can look for the solution to resolve it in the most beneficial way. Now Darrin does the opposite usually, he takes that chaos and defines the meaning with anger, frustration, more problems and most of the time uses blame to anyone involved or even not involved. So here we can clearly see the contrast of taking anything and giving it different meaning to it and then the energy vibration that goes along with it expands. Darrin would have a peaceful life if he acted with similar attitudes as Samantha.

When we take this information from science or true nature of reality to bring everything and anything back to its nothingness state then we come to realize that it is always up to ourselves in how we react with negativity like Darrin or respond positively like Samantha.

This is a massive difference on not only how things then evolve to turn out for our future and for our health and well being, this is the shift we are going through on our planet now. If we are more like Darrin it will take some work to create the shift in our lives because of the old conditioned way that has become such a reaction of a daily habit. This is where the power lies, in the awareness that it is a habit and that if we continually respond differently we will get different results.

So if we realize that everything is back to its original state of nothingness or neutral as a wave function and it is only the meaning to define what we give to everything and anything, then we are in a powerful state to change the ripple effect of our present and future. Bringing everything to a state of neutral or nothingness is bringing it back to a wave state that we can then transform that nothingness that has no defined meaning into the meaning we choose to give it and as we observe it long enough we then collapse the wave into a physical particle to be our physical experience.

When everything seems to fall apart, let me refer to my life as many reading this book may have gone through one or many of the same experiences that I created without realizing it. It was when I realized the validity of the wisdom in quantum states and though change is constantly happening we can ride the wave easier when we understand the benefit of the chaos.

Everything must fall apart as it does in a wave function before it can restructure itself again into a particle state of our physical experience.

At different parts of my life my relationship to my ex-husband fell apart into chaos that at the time because of habitual beliefs I perpetuated unconsciously at the time I gave the defined meaning of going through hell. I perceived and reacted to it all negatively and as problems that took me on a journey of going through stages of anger, frustration, disappointment, revenge and hate until I finally got to forgiveness that softened everything. I also realized now that back then there were many other chaotic experiences that I attracted because of my automatic habitual reactions as the time. So we can realize I was a bit more like Darrin. It was until I found the knowledge through books, as many of us have, that led me on my search and evolving growth of over twenty years that bit by bit started turning things around. My financial beliefs also fell apart when I became no longer employed as I was for twenty years, no income, and no security. Though there was also a twenty year span between my relationship falling apart and then my job. But you get the jest of it all.

Many may know of these experiences when everything falls apart and if we attach old beliefs of negativity to it we become depressed and perpetuate the chaos. We come to realize that we do create all of our reality whether we are aware of it or not, it is what is going on. It is always ourselves who are doing it by what we keep focused upon with our thoughts and feelings that create our expectations from our beliefs that also create our attitudes.

Now I know and realize through my experiences and have chosen another path of taking all chaos as a factual energy pattern that it must take when we go through major changes. It is breaking down of old beliefs systems that no longer serve us in our new ways of knowledge we have turned into our wisdom through our experiences, we then can see the proof.

In quantum states everything that is a solid particle has to become broken down into the minutest vibration of energy until all formation of the original solid particle is collapsed into a wave. Waves of vibration or energy then become non solid without form. Which gives us the power to perceive the chaos in its natural form of all broken apart back into the neutral nothingness again? This can be like our life seems when it's a mess. In the new beliefs that we have become wise to in our knowing, we then see that everything had to fall apart to create the new blueprint of change for it to become into a wave state. Then in that powerful wave state which is when we can choose infinite possibilities and when we do through our aware attention in observing, it then changes to become something else.

Now this is where the most powerful choices are and this is the point that makes all the difference in what we create it to be. If we react in the same old way then in that powerful wave state we are then choosing, our own choices. If we are not aware then we miss the important powerful part in the creating wisdom.

It is through our observation then that we create through the collapse of the wave to become of more solid negative creations or positive ones. If we react negatively then more negative experiences will become of our present and future and not so well being of health too. If we respond positively, as lovingly as we can then we will create more positive, loving experiences in the now and the future. This is going on minutely, all of the time, these states of solid particles breaking down and collapsing into neutral nothingness state and then reforming again in the waves then back into particles. We are always controlling or influencing by the way we observe through reacting or responding that is continuously changing the way reality is perpetually created.

If we continue to react negatively to most experiences then we will consistently see our life that way and create it the same if it's the opposite of positive or love. Though it is all energy the difference is profound on how it plays out in the creation of it in our lives.

The way to surely know if we are living the way we really love our life to be or not is to just look around to see if we like what we already have created as a result. If there are things we do not like we can realize that we did create it and have the power in the moment with it's momentum to change it by focusing and thinking better feeling thoughts. More in alignment with what we do want and consistently being aware and consistently changing our thoughts to have better feelings. Taking advantage of the wisdom of quantum states because that is what the nature of reality is.

Sure Darrin is happy some of the time but Samantha seems to be happy most of the time even through all the chaos she creates the situations to become more loving and positive for all involved. Well except for the very beginning of the first season when Samantha does become angry and does use revenge against Darrin's old girlfriend Sheila. We see that she learned very quickly to transform all that negativity to positive in the other seasons of the show. Samantha's new way she responds is a ripple effect to everything and everyone along the way, regardless she defines anything and everything to have the best end result by her constant observing nature.

Collapsing the waves back into nothingness a neutral state then back to creation of particles then back to waves then back to particles that keep breaking apart and coming together. It seems to be what we are doing every minute all day long and all our lifetimes too. When we become aware and transform our neutral nothingness to more loving ways to respond then our lives will also have happy endings just like in every Bewitched show. We can have a magical life by responding with loving positive joyful energy that will give the highest most beneficial meanings to define everything in our own lives. It will create a high vibration of ripple effect on everything and everyone.

CRAFT 15

+++++++++++++

TRUSTING EXPECTATION OF THE BEWITCHING POWERS

This part of the formula is the most powerful of the potion of what bewitching and creating reality in the most magical way because if we do not expect what we desire and trust it will be manifested, then we could be waiting a long time.

Throughout the shows some of the Bewitched family members have went to use their powers and nothing happened or it was altered of their expectations? Especially for Aunt Clara, she has become faulty in using her powers but of course the only reason is because she believes that aging is deteriorating her powers, which to me is a mortal belief. Aunt Clara seems to be the only one other then her old boyfriend who also believes as she does, the other members of the Bewitched family never seem to age. Recalling the episode of Darrin finding a picture of Samantha that Endora conjured up of Samantha being centuries old and never aging physically. Which stirs Darrin's thoughts to expect the worse for his future, but more about that in the aging chapter.

All the other family members just know and expect when they put they're intention out it just manifests just like that, whether it is a snap of the fingers, wiggle of the nose, waving of their hands, incantations or spells. Their power usually matches their intentions of expecting and trusting. So they feel and know it will work and then walla magically it transforms or creates or pops them anywhere they choose to go. Just like that, they do not expect it not to, they expect, trust and feel that their power and magic is always there when they go to use it.

This is the reason Bewitched became such a popular television show because when we watched it we loved the powerful and magical way that Samantha and her family lived. It is mirroring a powerful part in us that is still lying dormant awaiting us to start using. It's reflecting our own powerful natural self that really is magical. Especially when we see our lives as hum drum, bewitching shows us that life does not have to be so mundane. It can be showing us that a bewitching life can allow us some adventure and even Gladys next door wants in on it too, that is the reason she is so preoccupied with her neighbors. Magic just seemed to spark up the magic in all of us who enjoyed basking in that reality for a half hour of each day, bringing some spark to our own life through watching it.

When we realize that we all have the same magical power too except we have linear time gaps that prevent us from manifesting as fast as the Bewitching family. There are a small percentage of people on this planet that can manifest on command and what we are evolving to becoming for our future. Yet there are still the majority of people who still do not even realize that they create all of their reality and that is giving their power away. Whether we realize it or believe it or not, all one has to do is observe for a few weeks of how what we focus our thoughts on we become to feel about and speak about creates our own personal realities.

Since everything is energy, our thoughts, our words, our voice, our bodies, and everything physical all has energy vibrations. And the vibrations create frequencies that connect everything together and attract us to everything else, like a magnet. That is quite magical in itself. All we have to do is continue to focus on something we want and every time the want or desire pops in our mind then we think of it as we already have it. When we add some good feelings to our desire, focused thought then that feeling will fuel it all into motion. Then before we know it we will manifest it, receive it. When w remember that we are creating reality all of the time and always have been, it's just the illusion of the beliefs that don't allow us to see the true nature of reality working until we become aware.

We must expect it with trust and feel as if we already have it, that way Infinite Source, the Infinite Living Intelligence, our Creator and our vibration will keep us in the receivership mode. But if we add some doubt in the thoughts of it then we are pushing it further away, like a magnet resisting or pushing away. Or cancel it all together, it is dependant on our own self of how much pure expect trustful power we give our desire or wants. Just as Samantha expects and trust her powers is the same as we expect to breathe, it is so natural they don't even have to think about it. It's automatically accepted that her power is there when she uses it, that is expecting with trust. For our own selves because we are learning to use our magical powers with awareness, our magical powers could be perceived as the nature or reality in how we do create reality. This is what gives us our power back because once we realize and know for our own self, without any doubts, we just know it is the way it is, then we can control it. If we do not realize the truth in that then we believe we are powerless and that things, experiences just happen to us, like Darrin. When we take our power back in the realization that we do create all of our reality we become like Samantha. The more consciously aware that we become minutely of how we are creating reality the better we become at it until eventually the time gaps become less and less.

Unfortunately we were not born like Tabitha who is able to just naturally use her magic, for most of us we must lift from the amnesia that sets in when we are born. We must remember our powerfulness, our creativeness, our real true selves that we are, it is almost like a backward process compared to the Bewitched family.

Presently the children born with super powers that I wrote about in previous chapter are guided by their parents to not only use their powers but also expand to reveal more power that's available. They are being labeled as Super psychic children are doing similar things like the Bewitching family. If they can do all that and they are human or as the Bewitched family refers to as mortals then they are our role models too. Showing us what is possible for ourselves to do when we believe and practice long enough. Now that is bewitching! And this is where trust and expectation comes in, the more we become more comfortable in the accepting of our powers then the more we will trust and expect more to become for us.

How do we come to trust and expect a desire if we deep down do not believe we can experience or manifest it? For myself I have found that the more attention I give the thoughts as if I already have it especially when I add the feelings to it and then doing this repetitiously throughout each day. Ask yourself what would it really feel like if you were to already have what you want and play in it for awhile. What that does is get the emotions that are just scattered like fragmented pieces to stir together and attach to the desired thought and creates the feelings to be felt that is then creating in the process.

Let's use an analogy of your vehicle. When you know you have a full tank of gasoline, you start your vehicle as if you are starting your thoughts to attach to your desire. Then you put your foot on the gas petal and press all the way down, you can feel and hear the power but because you are still in PARK on your shifter you are staying in one place, going no where. This is similar to having a desired thought with scattered emotions, but once you take that shifter and move it from the park position and put it into drive, off you go. This can be perceived similar to your thought of desire and your scattered emotions are all fueled up but until you release that holding point into genuine feelings you will stay stuck in that momentum. This is the letting go stage after expecting and trusting.

At first it's easy to expect that it may feel doubtful depending on your own believability of whatever it is you desire. It's like being in park position for awhile, but after some practice it becomes more acceptable to even believe it is possible. Then it moves to a feeling of genuine knowing which transforms into a heart felt expecting and trusting the desire will be manifested or you will experience what you want. Just know it's on the way and getting closer and closer, then it eventually manifests or is experienced. As we have already gone over in other parts of the book, all our desires could be manifested immediately, it is our own beliefs that get in the way of that occurring.

So we must work by fine tuning our selves until we get to expecting and trusting it so that it can zoom right in. And take ourselves out of that park position to just go with it, expect and trust that you know it is just so close and let it go.

Believe, trust, expect and let it go knowing it's on the way just as you are on your way to your destination when you get into your vehicle to go somewhere. If you did not have a destination point to go to a certain location then you would just drive randomly and keep driving. Just as we need to align our desired thought and attach the feelings as if we know where we want to go and will arrive there, as a manifested desire will manifest. Just as you know that if you get into your vehicle put it in drive and your desire is to land up at the store, you expect, trust and feel that you will. You will get what you needed and return home. You do not expect not to arrive there or get to the parking lot and then go home without going in the store to come home without what you went there for to begin with. That seems to be what we do when we do not have the absolute faith of trust and knowing that we are on our way with our desires and know they are on its way to us. This is similar when we manifest what we do not want, the same as going into the store with a list and walk out with everything but what we desired originally.

This is the importance of using all the ingredients in our creating process of imagining or visualizations, words spoken because we know everything is adding energy to our desire. If we speak and feel untrusting of it then that is what will continue to manifest until we really perfect it with expecting trustful feelings as if we already know it is ours, the desire manifested. This is sitting in the receivership of it, waiting with absolute trustful knowing its on its way, so close.

Another analogy we could use is that you ordered a book on the internet and the seller said it would take two to three weeks for delivery. You accept that and give them your address to where you want it delivered. If you did not give them your exact address then the package would probably never arrive, it would get lost who knows where. If you put just your city and postal code that would zoom it in a bit more and probably be left at the post office of your city. Realize the differences here, if you put the exact number, street and your name and city, country and postal code, it will be delivered to your door if you used a delivery system that delivers to your door. Being precisely specific means everything in creating our reality deliberately, with awareness

This analogy can show us the variations of our desires and how we receive them. If we desire money but if we are vague on the amount and do not believe we are worthy of it or trust it will come to us, we are not being specific. It is just like not giving our exact address to the delivery, we are not giving enough specifics to have it received. But if we pick an exact amount and focus on it as if we already have received it especially with feelings and do it repetitiously removed from any doubt and continue to focus on it, we create the expectation and trust and letting go. Is the same thing as giving the exact address to receive the package, we give the exact details of what we want and then wait in the receivership mode. Just as we await and trust that our package will arrive at our home.

The whole of the combination, the whole of the equation all together of the creating process of consciously manifesting that aligns everything to collapse into the receivership of the desire

Observe and be aware of how you think and feel about you desire. The easier it is or becomes to naturally visualize and feel as if you are already living it or having it is how you will know how in tune you are with it. When you notice your desire becomes more natural and easy with no doubts then your accepting is tuning it in and getting clearer. Less static until the static is gone and all that is left is a clear feeling picturing of it as if you already have it or are it and you are giving heart felt thanks for it. Then you know you are a crystal clear channel for your desire to manifest, it is so close you feel like you can almost physically touch it and you just know you will. When you have enough repetition of your own proof of your manifestations it becomes recorded in your memory and becomes easier to trust, you expect it and just know. You become quite mastered at deliberately creating.

CRAFT 16

✝✝✝✝✝✝✝✝✝✝✝✝✝

WHAT? AN AGING WITCH?

AUNT CLARA OR SAMANTHA?

Since it is now proven through science, biology and the present most popular information shared by Bruce Lipton on how our bodies genes and DNA actually work. Our body does respond to how we respond to our environment, meaning it is the way we react or respond that our body gets the messages from and creates from those messages.

Even though Aunt Clara is a witch, have you ever wondered why she still believes in aging and deteriorating of her body and her powers? We have seen in some of the Bewitched shows that Samantha is over three hundred years old, or young. Aunt Clara's malfunctioning does add quite the adventurous flow to the shows comical side of it. But if we instead use Samantha's sustaining of her non aging body and powers to go with it, then we can expand our selves to connect the science of the new biology that proves we are what we think.

We are what we think about everything.

When we really know and accept that our thoughts are energy, our body is energy, then we realize that it is what we think that matters the most literally. Its not that we age physically that matters, it's about what we think about aging that matters., and how we react or respond to everything that seems to happen to us.

If every time we look in a mirror at ourselves and see our face aging with wrinkles, we become one with those aging thoughts. Our body responds exactly to what we think, if its thoughts that you are getting older on a consistent basis, that's how the body will create your appearance to be.

Instead if you were to look into the mirror and ignore those new wrinkles or even old wrinkles and see the wrinkles changing into new cellular skin, to become younger looking, this makes all the difference. It does not even matter at what age you start to do this, the body will respond at anytime you start to change your perception from your thoughts about it. If you were to do it every single time you looked in the mirror eventually you will start to see the outcome, the evidence of yourself looking younger. Your body will get the message, it always does in everything you tell it, or by what it picks up from your automatic unaware thoughts. you are the one in command and your body always receives the messages. The body only knows what to do dependant on what you tell it to do, that is it, the way it creates and performs it to be. Expect it to age and deteriorate and it will follow your commands. Tell it to reverse the aging process and it will do just that, reverse it to whatever age you command it to.

It's our own beliefs that we choose to accept that is the condition we agreed upon to age and deteriorate, it is not the truth. If it were true we would all age the same every year, and we can see that's not the truth.. We all seem to age differently and become to create gray hair at different ages, that should make us realize and see the truth of how powerful we really are. All from conditional beliefs someone else has created for us to believe in as truth, but if we are in tune with our true natural selves then we can create with awareness with our own desires. Letting go of those old stagnated beliefs and create new ones that are empowering for our selves. So that our bodies have new commands to respond to and create for our bodies to appear as.

Just as any power is, it is up to our own selves to create what we want, creating what we want or desire is the same for things we want objectively or subjectively. From within to become without is always the way everything works and manifests. Aging is the same way, we are desiring to manifest our body to grow younger instead of older. It is taking our power back and creating our bodies and lives the way we decide to have it, when we know we create everything. Being a conscious creator deliberately with creativity and no longer letting any other undesirable beliefs dictate to us how we should desire to create our reality. We know ourselves more then anyone else does once we accept our power for ourselves.

Let's refer to the episode when Darrin becomes so upset when he realizes that Samantha will never age. When he peaks into the future to see himself decades later how he will age and deteriorate and Samantha stays young, he allows himself to become worried and depressed about it. What if instead he realized to know how the body works and focused on how he can also be like Samantha and change his DNA by how he focuses and thinks about aging? Darrin would then feel empowered instead of depressed and feel more empowered once he started to actually see the proof for himself as his body starts to look and feel younger.

Darrin could see and feel in his inner mind first how he wants his body to appear by giving new messages by choosing to think younger thoughts. When we do the same thing, think and already see in our mind the youthful vibrant appearance already changing, it will change also how we view our self in the mirror.

It is your own observation that affects the reality you then see, the power is in you not outside you, inner first then outer. Do you desire your hair to grow in it's natural color? Then give it the attention which simultaneously will give your body cells the message and also then give the scalp and hair follicles, all that is needed to allow that command to become reproduced. It really is as simple as we allow it to be. The only time lapses is dependent on you own allowing of it to become, when you get passed the doubt into believability then into knowing and expecting with trust, it will just become the way you desire to be. Though it may not be easy in the beginning because of those old stubborn beliefs that you have valued for so long. However, with enough repetition of the new thoughts and feelings and doing it long enough to see your own proof it does become simpler. Then simpler becomes the natural way to choose to think and also see the results.

We must remind ourselves that this nature of reality wisdom goes for everything. What you think about what you eat, what you think about your body to be over weight or under weight or perfect weight. If you think that everything you eat is good for you and turns into nutrition then it will. It is always dependent on what you think about everything, you are the one that is always giving the commands.

When you realize that you are the one giving the command then you get your power back. It is when you allow beliefs that are disempowering and limit your wonderful fluid body and give them messages you want to be expressed through your body.

To prove this to your own self once and for all and not just take my experience of it but that it is all up to our own self in how you are appearing from the messages you give your self all of the time. You have the power to change anything, it is already in your divine DNA heritage. At anytime you can change old beliefs into creative commands that you prefer by repetitiously seeing the new you before the new you has appeared. Then before you realize it you will be staring into the mirror in wonderful delight at how powerful you really are, the new younger you staring back at you. That is refusing to be like Aunt Clara or Darrin and instead choose to be like Samantha.

CRAFT 17

+++++++++++++

THE CRYSTAL BALL
OF
ALL POSSIBILITIES

In the Bewitched heritage family, they do not need money because they can manifest anything and everything they ever could want, however in Darrin's reality which is still conformed to using money to get the things he wants. He must work at a job to earn a salary of money to live his life from that reality he is conformed to. If we were to take a peak into the crystal ball of our future if we evolve to becoming more like the bewitched family we would see many changes.

Since we would no longer have to work jobs to earn money, then what would we be doing? I suppose everyone would be doing what they wanted to do, what they enjoyed to do on a regular basis, what they loved to do. The individuals who really enjoyed their jobs would continue working doing the jobs but without any pay. It would just be a service to others like volunteer work is presently.

The things that we refer to as chores would also be obsolete because a chore could be done with the wave of our hands or a twitch of our nose. Even shopping would be a different experience, since we did not have to pay for anything, there would be no need for sales person at cashiers. Though if the individuals who enjoyed their work as a sales person they could be available if help was needed in the stores. But if no sales person was there we would just walk in and pick out what we wanted and leave with the items.

I know it does sound so outrageous considering a world as this, however if we evolved into it slowly it would not be such a shock put upon us. The slow pace of evolving would sustain the momentum to allow us to get comfortable with the new ways. Just as anything new seems outrageous compared to the old familiar perceptions or the way reality was to the new one.

We could list so many of these types of changes that eventually the majority did eventually conform to. One is when humans believed that the world was flat, it sounded outrageous and crazy to hear the possibility that the world just might be round. Some individuals feared that Columbus and his crew would fall off the end of the world. Columbus being courageously brave and passionate in his knowing of his Quest to follow his intuition and not be in fear as the others who judged him irrational or crazy. His intuition guided and inspired him to flow through any fears he may have had. Columbus believed in his intuition to accomplish his mission, which he did and it changed everyone's ideas of the world.

The discovery of the light bulb and electricity, the discovery of magnetism and radiation, the discovery of building cars versus horse and buggy, even to the discovery of money. Many centuries ago money was not used, people exchanged food and other things for services. I am quite sure that if we were to tell the people back then that money would take over they would also have thought it outrageous too or not possible.

Just imagine trying to explain our present day technology and the way we live presently to someone from five hundred years ago. They would be in such great disbelief considering their primitive belief system and how they were living, they would think we were some kind of witches or sorcerers.

Try to imagine it from their perspective, a box with people in it living their lives for all to see. They walked or road a horse and buggy, they went to bed usually when it became dark and woke when it became light, except for the exception of candles. They wrote with dirt until ink was discovered. There was no money, no telephones, no technology, no furnaces, no appliances, they had out houses. It was a completely different reality back then and when we go back into their reality to perceive for a bit we can see that our reality would seem insane or superstitious. Just as much of what I am writing about may still seem outrageous now yet in the future would be accepted.

So let us imagine then peaking into our present reality windows of our home from our centuries past relatives and how they would see us. They would see us sitting on a comfortable sofa all staring at a box with people appearing to live they're lives right in front of us. They wouldn't know what a TV program is or that these people are actors on a screen, not in the box, it is projected through a service provider, which some are satellites high in the sky projecting the signals.

If our distant relatives were to continue observing to watch us use a remote control and press buttons that change the channels on our box, they would think we were magical to be able to do that too. How crazy would that be like to a person from five hundred years ago? Seeing us cooking on a stove with the burner element heating up. A refrigerator that keeps things cold with a light in it and lights lit up everywhere in the rooms of our home, or to warm up a TV dinner in the microwave in seconds. And if they were to view our children in their rooms in front of a computer, no matter what they were doing on the computer it would appear as magic, especially if they were to see an images of who we were video chatting with. Then they watch us walk around with a gadget we put to our ear without any cords and can call anywhere in the world, but for them they would see it and probably question why are we talking to ourselves in that gadget. Or take a picture or video with a digital camera and then download to watch it with sound on our computer instantaneously. If they were to observe us send a fax, what would they think we were doing? Then watch us use a remote car door opener, they would see us press a button the garage door lift up we drive out of it in a vehicle. Then the garage door closes and we drive to a store where everything is in it and we give a card to the person behind the counter. First the store would seem outrageous and confusing, let alone giving a card to the another person and then walk out with bags of stuff. Our distant relatives would be similar to Gladys in Bewitched show observing everything that is going on with the Bewitching family. She witnesses herself but is made out to be crazy to everyone else but the Bewitched family that goes along with it so that their secret is kept from everyone else.

Just imagine how magical and bewitching this would appear to our distant relative considering they were still watching because by now they may have thought they were going crazy or stumbled into an alien reality of superstition and maybe even some evilness depending on their beliefs. Remember they are coming from a reality that this would all seem like superstition and magic, how else would they be able to comprehend our reality to compare to their reality? Considering only what they know to be true.

So we would appear as magical and bewitching to them as any other alien reality would appear to us now. So now let us imagine that we are the same as the past relative who was peaking into our reality like Gladys does, but we are peaking into a future reality from our now present moment. Are you ready for the adventure?

Good lets go! As we peak into the home of a future reality from us we see four family members sitting on a sofa watching a screen that is wall size, it covers one whole wall. As we watch and listen it appears that the family is wishing another family Merry Christmas but they are asking how is the weather on Venus? Which the reply is good, how is the weather on Earth? The conversation continues with one relative from Venus to pop in here for an hour or so, then next thing we watch is the person pop out of existence from sitting on the sofa. Then instantaneously appear on the big screen sitting now with the family on Venus and the conversations continue.

To us it would also look bizarre and freaky and we'd probably be quite superstitious of it just as our past relative from 500 years ago perceived us in our present. However to the individuals in this reality they have already mastered teleporting, which to us is prehistoric, how would our beliefs comprehend it?

As we continue to watch we see a few bowls of popcorn pop from thin air onto the coffee table, then the individuals take the bowls and start eating the popcorn.

As we further observe we watch them change the channels on the wall screen not with a remote but with a pointing of they're finger, as they are using their telekinesis abilities. Then we observe one of the parents tell the others they are going out for awhile and we watch him go into what appears as a fly saucer type vehicle. Instead of it driving down a road, it flies up in the air like a plane. Then we wonder why they even have these saucer vehicles when they can pop anywhere they want to go, we assume it is because they just want to travel that way, maybe it is nostalgic.

We also notice that there are roads in the air, looking more like the Jetson's, remember that old cartoon show we watched when we were kids. As we go back to observing in the house we notice a big machine and one of teenagers goes into it and says to her mother, "I will be back later I am going to visit grandpa for awhile." As we listen into the conversation with the mother and the teenage boy that is still on the sofa, we are really startled. As they explain how great it is that the veils have finally thinned, how in past history they're ancestor were terrified to die as they're beliefs back then were so limited.

The mother goes on to explain to her son how back in day of the past that they did not have a machine to visit the people who died, so he should really appreciate all the things he has now.

In their reality there is no such thing as lack or survival or even sadness. If they miss someone who died they can go visit them in their time machine with a few pressing of some buttons and vise versa anyone who died can visit them in their reality too.

If we really allowed our creativity and leaped into many more possibilities of what a future world would be like we would be quite amazed. I truly believe that these other dimensions of realities are going on and have always been going on. It is all dependant on how passionately we really want to know, which takes expanding our consciousness into other realms.

Just as if we traveled to Paris from Canada we would then know and experience Paris, but if we never traveled and went to Paris, we assume Paris is there but just never experienced it. Unless we watched it on a television program, but if we did not have that type of technology then we would only have to take someone else's truth of it. Just as quantum physics is setting the ground for our future to evolve, urging humanity to be more and more comfortable with other dimensional realities. Bit by bit we expand our limited beliefs to become a bit more accepting of what we just couldn't accept decades ago. Quantum physics is showing us that if we even think it then we have picked it out of infinite possibilities that already exists, because how could we even think it if it did not exist in the quantum field of infinite consciousness.

So I hope that I stirred some of the magical brew of our crystal ball to expand your mind of how perceptions can differ and expand into the unknown to get us to ponder to get to know more of the unknown. No one can deny that the infinite possibilities are still unknown to most because unlimited consciousness just has such a hard particle type of frame of linear mind to comprehending the collapsing waves of infinity. One must have to peak out further past the rational judging mind that limits by fear of the unknown. But bit by bit as some leading edge individuals like Columbus ride that leading edge for the collective consciousness to follow, it will make it easier to accept and eventually evolve to follow for our future.

CRAFT 18

++++++++++++

DARRIN OR ENDORA?

WHO'S YOUR ROLE MODEL?

Let us revise the comparison between the two individuals that are in each others realities yet living their own realities. Darrin is conformed to the limited reality establishing to control Samantha using love as his leverage. Instead of the other way around that Darrin could choose to expand himself and join in the adventures in a different way. Darrin could of said to Samantha, wow, this is great, how can I become more as your heritage and family to make life more blissful and easier for us. Then instead of trying to control Samantha with stresses and guilt for using witch craft which is her natural abilities. Darrin then would be allowing Samantha her birth rite and she as a role model for him to become. Instead he choose to manipulate Samantha and punish her with his non acceptance with his anger sprouting tantrums of his limiting reality. Though I admit it did create many varieties of adventures an I am quite sure left most of us screaming at the television saying, "Get a life Darrin and leave Samantha alone!"

What a different show it could have been if we imagine the show being changed to Darrin actually conforming by accepting the Bewitching family's heritage. If Darrin instead used their role modeling to be the first mortal to evolve to learning and using the powers that are available within mortals. We would have had a show that would of inspired us to wonder more into our divine heritage. Watching Darrin learn and use his powers and all the challenges and mishaps that he would of went through as he perfected his mastering of his powers. Then imagine Gladys watching all that was going on.

For now we will use the show as it was created and compare Darrin's reality and beliefs and life to Endora. We see that Endora has the most fun. She can do everything, be anything, go anywhere have anything. She is a free sovereign being that no one gets in her way, she chooses consciously to never alter her blissful magical life, ever. Though she likes to have fun with Darrin and perpetually tries to show Samantha how ridiculous she is being to marry a mortal and letting Darrin make the rules to control her.

So truthfully ask yourself, if you had the chance and knew there was even a fractional possibility to be like Darrin or Endora, who would you choose to be?

Believe it or not this is a very important question, as the answer will create your destiny to stay humdrum and controlled or sovereign and own your own self, which of course has been your real true destiny all along.

To stay like Darrin is to allow the media and anyone in authority to dictate to you what is true. Take a look at the epidemic that went on with the flu shots. People standing in line for hours to get a vaccine because they have been tricked into believing in a fear that was conjured up to sustain more fear. If anyone uses fear for suggestibility to others, we must take the spells off ourselves to see what is really going on behind these illusions. How hypnotized have we allowed ourselves to be? Suggesting in fear that if you do not get a shot your chances of catching the flu may kill you. Is that not a threat? It sure is a threat to use fear to control individuals who are easy too control, the same as using a hypnotic suggestion knowing the other individual is very easy to hypnotize.

It's true fact that individuals were put under hypnosis and told that a lit cigarette was held to their skin and burning their skin. It was not a cigarette but pencil. Yet the individuals under hypnosis did not know it, they were hypnotized which is a trance state, like a spell of allowing another to give a suggestion and then the person follows the suggestion and their body responds. That is similar to how Endora puts Darrin under her hypnotic spells that Darrin is probably always in fear of the next situation he believes he has no control over.

How much proof do we need to realize that fear only is a tool to suggest to people that believe in what authority dictates to them instead of believing in themselves. When an individual does not believe in their own self they are suggestible to any one else that dictates any suggestions, which shows they are still in fear. Then fear is used to stimulate reactions if not followed, then the suggestions made by others will be what the individuals will follow and believe in.

An Endora type of sovereign individual will know that they trust themselves and no amount of fear is going to alter that self trust. They work with their own mind, beliefs, power in sustaining or creating their bodies to function in their commanding responses, not anyone else's. They would not be standing in line for a shot, they would be too busy working on themselves and evolving to becoming fully sovereign onto themselves. To become a role model for others to follow if the others were ready to let go of authority that tries to scare them into all these beliefs to begin with. If you are one of those individuals then never judge yourself for your present state. Instead just becoming more wise to how the nature of reality works and how your present state is always an opportunity to transform if you so desired to. If not then that is also your own free will to choose. It will never be wrong or right, it will always be a choice in any lifetime to take your power back. Especially when we take our Power Back and become more like Endora.

What are Some of the Illusions that are Wrapped up in Old Beliefs?

If we were to no longer allow any other to steal our power. Just as Gladys is so curious and loves being nosey or is she really just being curious and wants to know more? Yet she is so stuck in her stubborn beliefs but then not as stuck as her husband. When we become open minded to want to know more about how our thoughts create our reality we work from a different process then following any authority's dictating. Especially when fear is the motivation that is being used to force or persuade us to do things that are not true to begin with or resonate with ourselves.

If your are to ask yourself the question, "what if you get the flu?" What is the first thoughts that pop into your mind about that question? But if you know that it is up to what your thinking is all about that brings harmony back to your body from any disharmony or dis-ease to begin with. You know that your thoughts originally are what created any dis-ease originally, whether you allowed another to suggest fearful thoughts or your own attachment to fearful thoughts. It's always up to your own self never anyone else's. It is even an illusion that allows a belief to believe that virus or anything can be contagious. Nothing is contagious, it is the illusion that gives the appearance that it is that way. In real reality it is the belief that gives the power and the command to the body, not any supposed infectious person to touch another person, or cough on another person. It is the person being coughed on and to whether they believe things are contagious. If they believe in that truth then the body will respond from that thought given command that when anyone who appears to be sick comes in contact with the other they will catch it. It is the belief of the attached thoughts that creates the body to command in response from as a created result to then appear as it just happened.

So again we must ponder further into questioning because being like a Darrin will be you giving your god given creator's powers away every single time. Being like Endora will bring you to sovereignty returning all your power back to your own self, always. The way life will flow to be created will be as a rippling domino effect from that point onward and can make all the difference.

It's the unaware allowing of yourself to stay or be hypnotized to others suggestions especially if it is out of fear based energy compared to your own suggestions to be one of love for your own self. When we truly with our own sovereignty love ourselves we no longer are triggered by fear because fear never sustains love and is the reason so many individuals break free from any type of abusive relationship. Usually without the awareness that their own energy did attract themselves to that destiny to learn, grow and evolve to not allowing any other to ever take their power away again.

Once we perceive from that powerful point of perception then we never alter our blissful love for anyone or anything. We are so connected with our true natural self that nothing can tip us from that loving being we are. Instead of seeing the fragmented pieces of a scattered picture we then see the whole of the picture, which is seeing through fear illusions and seeing real love.

We then realize that the quest in that journey of the question, are we going to stay like the Darrin or evolve to become like Endora?

Pondering and answering the question can be a powerful destiny life changing journey. Allowing the Darrin in us all to break free from Endora's spells, just like breaking free from fearful authority's suggestions. Your destiny is then not some future reality that just comes about on it's own. It comes about dependent on the changes that are made in the powerful present moment by moment that gives either a new momentum or an stalemate old one to continue.

So I hope this leads your path of walking through the fearful dungeon of believing you are a victim to instead turn on the lights. Awaken to realize that the path of broken hypnotic spells that kept you so limited in conformed conditioning can stretch into the expanding unknown to known. To shine the light in all the dark beliefs that you desire to transform.

Knowing the choice is always up to our own selves to break free like Endora or stay in the dark confused reality as Darrin. Darrin is stuck because he believes everything just happens to him and he believes he has no control over his life. Compared to Endora, she choose to have all the power and control, allowing her destiny to unfold by focusing on her own desires with intention and trusts she knows it's the way. Endora never predicts her future, she creates it by her beliefs in herself. Just as we could as it would leads us to be opened to many other creative doors of all possibilities to be known for the choosing, to create an evolving destiny to unfold in being created. It is then doing it our way, we then are wise of the statement, " I Am."

Real Bewitching Things that are Going on Presently

Here I would love to share a prime example that will show us our true potential that is available to us. Whether you yourself have had the direct experience with someone you know or even are a person who has multiple personalities. Now for psychologist they see these types of experiences for themselves because of the many individual patients they treat.

A most genius and respectable Canadian psychologist Dr. Lee Pulos who has written books that he shares and explains many of the extra ordinary experiences he has not only witnessed but has also courageously tried himself. I must admit myself that I have not witness this however years ago the idea of the ability to change eye color popped up in my mind to ponder about. Again Bruce Lipton discoveries in biology and the unlimited possibilities of our gene's and bodies DNA of creating from what we think and believe is now becoming proven science. So if you have not already read or heard about this information it's a great starter of evidential data of proven information.

When we give some thoughts to ponder about individuals who have multiple personalities and what they can do so automatically within seconds, it's really astonishing. This is physical proof that other individuals are manifesting immediately, even if they are not aware that they are doing it. In many cases these individual of multiple personalities actually do not remember when they switch personalities from one to another. But they can be our potential role modeling for us to know what possibilities we can also do when we let go of the hypnotized conditioned memories of beliefs of what we cannot do.

These individuals who experience multiple personalities can be in a state of being in one personality and have a disease as lupus and stutter while engaged in that one personality. Then within seconds, like a switching of a light switch on and off, they can switch to another state of being. Another personality who is confident and within seconds they no longer stutter, they no longer have any disease of the other personality they just experienced being. These individual's eye color will change to match the other personality from brown eye color in one personality to blue in another, instantaneously, with only a few seconds of a time lapse, which is almost instantly.

How much proof do we need to know that these things are occurring for those individuals immediately and then we have to wonder why we create long time lapses before we can manifest what we want. It is our own selves that create the delays and detours of what could be immediate manifestations of what we desire. So then of course we ask what does time have to do with manifesting? Actually nothing except for how we set it up by our own beliefs. How much deleting from limited suggestions do we need to do to releasing our held old stubborn beliefs that has become so limited to what is possible? When these multi personality individuals show us not only that it is possible but how they are doing it right now.

How do they do it?

It seems that researchers are only scratching the surface on theories of how it could be possible. Dr. Pulos theorizes that it may be that they protrude. Now what does that mean? It means that these individuals are able to be in a neutral void, released of any conditioning or suggestions to say what they cannot do these things. They can automatically do these things because they believe it is not themselves doing it. They think it's another individual, yet they are the same individual with different personalities.

What's really amazing and important is how they do it if we are to reciprocate the same manifestations yet in a natural healthy way. This expands ourselves to evolve in consciousness and experience it in physical for our own selves. This would then be a controlled desire to manifest as I had stated of my desire to change my eye color. I would then be doing it consciously with the inspiration to experience it to evolve my consciousness in physical embodiment to experience our powerful divine nature.

Dr. Lee Pulos explained that one individual was completely medically confirmed as blind yet in another personality shift within seconds had perfect 20/20 eyesight. Amazing and true. How powerful are we, very powerful absolutely.

What Other Possibilities are Also Available?

Hair growing in our natural color instead of gray as is now believed as normal while aging. Not for vanity reasons but for being able to experience it as an amazing ability, to experience the more that we can do with the wisdom we discover. If many became to accomplish this and it evolved into collective consciousness then it would be a natural occurrence. Just as the normal beliefs of gray growing in with age or stress is presently accepted. I am sure that everyone knows someone in their senior years that still has their natural hair color and never had gray hair grow in. Usually it's chalked up to heredity somewhere down the genetic line.

Presently there are individuals on this planet that can levitate their bodies. Some can insert 5 inch knitting needles through their hand with their mind by seeing the hand as it really is, which is energy. Tolly Burkan has been doing seminars of this for decades.

Many individuals, myself included travel out of body and have the proof that they do it with much evidence, one being by traveling out of body and remote viewing. Tom Campbell gives many experiences and information about OOB as he as been doing it for decades. We can be in a friend's living room and then call the friend to confirm what the friend was actually doing.

Another ability I already described in other crafted chapters is moving objects without physical touch, just using intention and energy, we refer to this as telekinesis. In the Philippines' and Brazil and many other locations throughout the world, as Dr. Lee Pulos again not only talks about but has had the actual experience of healers putting their own hands through individuals skin as if it was just water. Shirley McClaine has done the same, but at the time many just could not accept that these things were possible, just as Shirley and Dr. Pulos did not either and was the very reason they went in person to see it for themselves. It seems that anyone who experiences it for their own self as proof is profoundly changed by it. It's such a expansion of consciousness that instantly old beliefs just crumble away. No matter what another or any skeptical person believes or thinks, if they are to do it themselves they would no longer be skeptical.

So just because it is going on all around the world and still most of the population are not aware of it, or believe it, is only because they are not interested. Just as any neighbors that live on the street where Darrin and Samantha lived, the neighbors except for Gladys and Abner, did not know of anything that was going on in the Bewitched home. Just as skeptics are staying in the limited thinking reality when there is so much expansion of unlimited possibilities to know and experience. I believe this is all part of our evolution to becoming more spiritual in our physical bodies. To continue to expand our consciousness and create new beliefs from our own experiences that break through the illusions of limitations of what is possible. It is the journey we are on now and more and more are waking up to it, even though still the larger part of our planet has not yet. It is the one's who are doing these things, practicing these things that are on the leading powerful edge to evolve the rest to eventually become to evolve through the process.

We could use an analogy and compare all of this to a satellite server. With a satellite server we have available to us to receive hundreds of channels but what if we choose to watch one channel?

Considering all those frequencies of programs are available for us to watch. So watching one channel is limiting, yet that is what many are doing now in reality when so many channels or realities of possibilities are going on all over the world. Others are doing what seemed impossible but they are doing it. It is up to ourselves to also practice using those incredible individuals as a role model to have our own experiences. By doing and experiencing what seemed impossible to the limited rational mind and expand it to do more.

Allow ourselves to creatively imagine what other possibilities there is for us to do. If we can conceive of anything that means it is there in the infinite field of possibility already because it was imagined. With infinite realities going on simultaneously nothing is impossible. So let us do that right now, let us think what is possible. We already have glimpses of what is going on around the world now that seem impossible to most but is being done now by others.

Let's give more thought about reverse the aging process by learning about the brain and the true biology of the body cells and DNA and genes in our body. Everything that Channeler's and other masters have been saying for eons is now being proven to be scientifically true.

Knowledge of multiple personalities allows us to realize that so many idea's we may have thought were outrageous, crazy and impossible are possible. How fantastically amazing is that?

Then we must wonder once we have delved into the nature of reality and how everything is energy and we are connected to everything whether its another or objects? Effecting objects like vehicles, appliances, are we are doing it all of the time but without the awareness that we are doing it? Yet we have collective beliefs that dictates for us and we expect things to deteriorate with age. What is the difference when we transform those old beliefs to new ones? Ideas as that allows unlimited thoughts to take over those old limiting beliefs so that everything will become in alignment with the new knowledge. That would expand our consciousness to see behind many illusions that we have put value to believe in presently. It would be that your vehicle will be what you think it is, your appliances will also conform to your own energy and expectations, as everything is connected, everything. Energy is energy. Our hearts and thoughts unite in everything we create even though we may not see all the connections because of our limiting perceptional views.

As the paranormal as in bewitching abilities starts to become normal through our own experiences and it is just our perception that changes. We then can perceive things in a more expanded way which then allows us to do many seemingly impossible things to be possible now for us.

On a radio show I listened to from 'news for the soul talk show' that Nicole Whitney founded, I listened to Nicole and Dr. Lee Pulos as he spoke about children all over the world who have not been conditioned into believing what they cannot do. Dr. Pulos spoke about a child in Japan that stopped an escalator with his mind's energy, others who teleported objects into another room by actual teleportation. Which means by their own energy and intention was able to move things by teleporting, which is popping objects into reality from seemingly nowhere.

Let us remind ourselves that we really cannot debunk this information just because we cannot yet wrap our minds around knowledge to comprehend Infinity. So much of our space time on this planet is filled with time which is very limiting. It would be like a grain of sand on a ocean beach and even that is probably a limited analogy for us in trying to comprehend forever of infinity. Only because of limited linear time in the space continuum of the infinite because of old beliefs we valued for maybe too long. Bit by bit, surely we can expand into unlimited if we allow our selves to think outside the box of what is referred to as normal and accept some of the paranormal.

Connecting with other multiple selves, many are doing it and Bruce Goldman has been doing it for decades and now teaches it for others to do. Again the possibilities are endless as far as infinity goes.

CRAFT 19

++++++++++++

FEEDBACK OF A
BEWITCHING LIFE IS
EVOLVING

In science whenever a scientist or whoever comes up with theories, first they experiment until they have enough proof that evaluates validity getting the same results from all who continue to experiment with the original experiments. This is their feedback to know that if one can do it and have similar results and others can too, then it is quite valuable, creditable and proven enough to bring it to the mainstream or public. Then the norm accepts it as fact and true and incorporates it and we live those facts in our lives. Then there is a minority just as you may be a part of this minority that resonate with information from masters other then science fact first. Science is a slowed down confirmation of what most of us that have learned about the nature of reality have already come to known. Through our own personal experiments in our lives, we already see proof from our own feedback.

Especially if we are lovers of the bewitched show, star trek, star wars, sliders and all or any of the so called fictional shows that were only preparing everyone for our future. What is really amazing is that in the process of our observing these shows which we only assumed we were just watching, we were actually having an affect, the "observer effect."

It's so interesting when we think about it? So let us think about this more in depth to really realize the substance of it all because it overflows into every single thing in not only our world but other dimensional realities too. That would mean that every movie or show or conversation or actually anything we ponder or watch or "observe" is having some kind of effect on something.

In watching shows like Bewitched we are effecting our future because we are observing it. Quantum physic's experiments show the results as of the "observer effect." In definition this means whatever we have our attention on, we affect the outcome. Not only the duration of the show we watch or observe but also it will pop up in many forms throughout our days, whether we are aware of not.

If we encounter something challenging to do we may think about how great it would be if bewitching were true, then we could just wave our hands with our desired intention and all the dishes would be done and put away. All one has to do is observe long enough of our own thoughts for awhile to see it reflect back to us, we will see the proof, that is guaranteed. However most of the time what we desire, as an example to have all the dishes done and put away will not be manifest for our experience exactly as we desired. Firstly because our beliefs are still too structured to support the kind beliefs needed for telekinesis. Really think about it, deep down how much of our belief system is engrained for that type of ability to be performed? Probably for most of us that means not very much at all. Sure we may have that desire however we have no memories of beliefs to support it to be able to experience it. What we will notice is our desire may becomes manifested in other ways that we do believe can manifest, like you mate wanted to surprise you and did all the dishes. Or someone else did the dishes for you and put them away. Or you went to dinner and had all the work done for you. There are many variable varieties of ways that our desire will be fulfilled in it's manifestation, however not exactly as we wanted it. However it's more in alignment with how we believed it would be. That is the reason behind the statements we don't always get manifested to us exactly what we desired. Even if we did imagine it would be the bewitching way. It's our beliefs of memories that have to be able to support the desire to manifested that way first. This is when practicing new abilities can make the difference because when we practice something long enough until we can experience something that seems impossible then we are creating a better supporting beliefs system that creates it to manifest specifically.

Let us use some hindsight in the mix and for an example let say you do play or watch violent shows or games and then something happens to you that is of the fear energy, as maybe your car was stolen. Now most do not connect the dots that observing is actually participating by our focused attention in watching a violent show or playing a violent or fear based game. In literal actuality, the nature of reality we are creating by observing and effecting an experience to become created in our personal reality. It may not be exactly as the show you watched or the game you played, however if it was of violence, we must remember that under the illusion of violence is the energy of fear. Since observing is participating and affecting since everything is energy and constantly creating reality, and when we start to connect the dots by being more aware of our reality we will see the evidence in some way.

If you think this is too spooky and outrageous to be true, yet something about it does resonates a deep heart felt feeling that most ignore, which of course is denial and stunts our evolutionary growth. If you are not paying attention or being more aware of how your reality is being created by what you are observing and doing then it will just appear in the illusion that everything just randomly happens. Yet remember that is only a false illusion not the nature of reality. Or unless you have already learned that from your own experiences that it is absolutely true and you have seen enough evidence of it in your own life as you became so aware. That is when we become to be very picky on what we put our attention on, whether it is in what we watch, listen to, because anything we put our attention on in every way is the observer effect and is effecting our lives and the collective consciousness of our planet and other dimensional realities too. This give us tremendous responsibility and great power to be aware of and to use in the most highest beneficial ways. This also perpetuates our evolving nature to create only the experiences we do want, personally and collectively.

Now let us also ponder a few minutes on the quest of the wondering of where did all these amazing, fascinating, so called fictional ideas arise from?

A great question with the answer already contained in it, as the paradox is that the QUEST of question has the other part of it in it with the " ion" at the end of the word. And what does "ion" define? Let us take a look. Wikipedia's "ion"definition: "to be considered an ion, they must carry a positive or negative charge. Thus, in an ionic bond, one 'bonder' must have a positive charge and the other a negative one. By sticking to each other, they resolve, or partially resolve, their separate charge imbalances. Positive to positive and negative to negative ionic bonds do not occur. (For an easily visible analogy, experiment with a pair of bar magnets." So we can see that the word "QUESTION" has two powerful words in it's whole word. As we separate our questioning into the first part of the word is our QUEST a desire to find or explore something. And in the last part of the word that has "ION" we realize that it is already bonded with the other part which it the answer. So we quest in the form of questioning that always leads us to the "ion" of the answer, no matter what journey we take to get or receive the answer, the answer is in the question. I thought that was very interesting to know since we are always wondering and questioning everything.

Okay now we can get back to the original last question, where do all these fascinating fictional ideas come from? If you already answered it with the blending of the quantum field, you already know you are so correct, absolutely. The quantum field is filled with infinite data and information and parallel realities, infinite dimensions of realities and in that quantum field it is void of time and space. There is no linear perception in the way that we think of past, present and future. Infinite has everything all occurring at once, simultaneously. Our linear time is a frame work, slowed down in vibrational frequencies for us to create and learn from our creations. So we can learn in our physical embodiment and experience to know the real nature of all reality and how we fit into it all. It is our feedback loop, the frame work to perceive the past as back then, experiences already experienced, which is only memories of the experiences.

The future as something we assume has not happened yet, and the present to get to know the difference. As Eckhart Tolle teaches in his books about "The Power of Now" and how if we are not in the present now we are really missing the incredible power of our selves. So this is where focus and attention come in when we are in absolute focus with our attention we are in the powerful quantum field of infinity. Even if in our powerful now we are thinking about past or future from memories in consciousness or memories in our soul's recording. Yet we are doing it in real time of Now and effecting those memories like a rippling wave affect and affecting everything else too. We come to realize that in any focused attention we put ourselves in, aware of or not, we are swimming in the quantum field of infinite consciousness of memories. Picking up information infinitely about anything we could ever imagine and more. We are picking up on future entities, past entities the variety is truly endless. Just try to comprehend a slice of infinity? We really cannot with our limited beliefs and mind, but bit by bit we grasps some concepts to try to come as close as we can to expand ourselves to desire to know more of it.

So yes that is where all the fascinating seeming fictional ideas are coming from, we and everything is connected to this infinite quantum field and always has been. We are connected literally to everything and everyone at some point in time of space in a momentum that takes expanding evolving consciousness to comprehend. But we are getting there slowly but surely. We are as we see from our own feedback how much we continue to keep changing.

Now we can clearly see how essential our feedback is personally for our own self and in life and science. More importantly to all dimensions of reality, infinitely, because everyone is always picking our of the quantum field, or infinite consciousness and growing and learning from it perpetually.

CRAFT 20

+++++++++++++

EVOLVING TO CREATING

NEW BETWITCHING WAYS

Let us take a look at the old ways of beliefs that we have been creating up to now and then we will be able to see the comparisons from both perceptions and the validity of the new way opposed to the old way. Let us also keep in mind that the "A" would be how Darrin lives his reality and the "B' would be how Endora lives her reality.

We must also realize that in our present reality we have already become very instantaneous in the way we are living our lives. Externally we can have debt to get what we want now and pay for it later, we can take medication and experience the side effects later or even create a new belief system that would allow us not to be affected with any side affects at all.

We can instantly take pictures with a camera or with our cell phone and download them onto our computer to store and view and share. Or not even download them now with all the new app's we can share then instantly. We can instantly talk to another through phone or computer and if we have the technology we can even see them while we speak or write to them. Instant letter writing would be the way an ancient ancestor may perceive emailing.

We are already living in a magical world of reality, however many of us do not even realize it or appreciate it enough to ponder the magical way we live compared to even only thirty years ago. It is so magical if it were to be perceived by an ancient relative that passed on but peaked into our world now. From horse and buggy to jet planes, from listening only to radio programs to television and recording programs when not even at home to view later when it is convenient for us. Appliances and technological gadgets that would surpass what any ancient relative would be able to comprehend to even make any sense of this futuristic world we live that they would view through their perceptions. This gives us a sense of how fast we have already externally evolved in just over thirty years.

We should keep in mind that all of these external technologies we now use first came as ideas from some mind and then became external for our uses, not the other way around. Just as all external realities become always first from the mind then manifested outwardly externally.

So now let us take a look at the comparisons below to perceive it as a future self would also view it not from a prehistoric past relative.

Old Mortal Way of a Job

In the old way we must train at a profession to get a job to make a income which the majority then works for someone else and receives a pay check for their services which is usually very limited to their real worth. They are also limited and must play by the rules of the employee without much opinion in the company. It would be viewed upon as being slave like and victimized in compared to the bigger evolved picture of reality. If we do not love what we are doing as a job then our body will also start to break down because the love is not there and instead can become to dread dragging our self to work.

New Bewitching Way of a Job

In the new way we would do what we love to do and be of a greater genuine heartfelt service for what we do. When we do what we love we are then passionate about what we are doing because we love it and that passion not only keeps us inspired to continue to do the best at it but also keeps us healthy. Health and love and passion goes hand in hand. The more you are passionate and love what you are doing the flow of money become staggering and ever abundant in multiple ways, instead of just one income, you can have many incomes to receive.

Old Mortal Way of Health

Many turn to doctors and medical professionals, as they have become to be labeled in description for not only advice but trust that they will fulfill the ill individual back to health. Usually by prescribing medication to bring the ill individuals body back to balance or harmony. This again is playing the role of the victim and being enslaved to another who you put your trust to do for you what you believe you cannot do. You are the victim and the doctor is dependant upon to be the savior, which is of course giving our power away to another and allow ourselves to be dependant upon them for our health. This is called the medical profession. Then being in denial of what the medications have as side effects so often becomes not even pondered upon. What it really comes down to is being disempowered from your own self.

New Bewitching Way of Health

The new way is to have as much knowledge as possible, which now there is massive amounts at our finger tips to learn from, however all that knowledge can only become wisdom through our own experiences and practicing of it. We become to know what we really are in physical embodiment and we come to know how our body and brain function. We connect the body as a way of communicating to us what we are out of harmony with our thoughts and beliefs that we feel and our body will communicate back to us what is going on. Pain is only a communication to let us know where our thoughts became out of harmony and the body is reacting to the thoughts and beliefs, we then get the feelings of those thoughts. If we are thinking out of our natural harmony of joy and love then the body will react to the feelings and then communicate some type of pain, discomfort until it becomes a disease if it is not being taken. It is the only way for the body to communicate to get our attention to watch what we are focusing our thoughts upon that is the only way the body can react. If your thoughts are harmoniously natural to your natural higher self of joy, love, regardless of what you may be going through in your daily life, then the body would never react in any pain or disease. Dis-ease of the body is exactly what is shown in the word, to be "dis" broken away from the "ease" which shows the hidden meaning in the word itself.

So in the new way if we felt any discomfort or pain, we would not react in victimhood of fear, we would respond as the body is telling us something and we would them realign our thoughts back to ease and then there would be no more discomfort that would continue to create any disease. When we get the messages clearly at the beginning of any discomfort then we no longer follow that path to create any further enfoldment to get more of our attention. So we no longer would need medial care, as it is termed, quite a trickery of a definition. I am not dishonoring the beautiful care that many professional medical workers do give to people, the whole point is not to judge them because if they knew this truth they would also be doing their jobs differently. So the whole point here is to see through the illusions to the way the body does function and how thoughts are always the creator of our body. To highlight the essentials of the knowledge and how we can become back in power of our own body by experiences that will allow us the wisdom to know the differences.

Old Mortal Way of Practicing

The old way of practicing until we are perfected at whatever we are learning to get so good at it so it becomes natural. We presently are still at this point in evolution because we are still only using a small percentage of our brains capacity. Especially when we are doing something that is unknown to us, whether it is learning to play an instrument or a sport, or manifesting an object out of thin air, we believe we need to practice. Hours and hours a day if we really desire to become perfected in our ability to do what we want. This takes large amounts of time of practicing to perfect because we are creating new wiring in our brains each time we practice, we are actually hardwiring our brain. So through our practicing at the beginning of whatever we choose to perfect, we are not very good. However as we continue to practice each time we get better and better at it until we finally are so good we have mastered it.

New Bewitching Way of Practicing

The new way will be to eliminate the need to practice, instead we will desire to do something and all we need to do is focus on it into the quantum field, or infinite intelligence mind and it will automatically be processed to us. So for example if we want to play the piano, all we do is purely focus and we will tap into the energy of a great piano master and then sit at the piano and just simply play beautiful music. This will be the same with anything we desire to experience whether it be playing an instrument, a sport or manifesting objects from thin air.

Old Mortal Way of Traveling

The old way is that we travel by placing our bodies into a vehicle of some sort, be it a car, plane, jet to get us from where we are to where we desire to go. It takes us time relative to the vehicle we choose to use and the time we have available to get to our destination.

New Bewitching Way of Traveling

The new ways would allow us to travel from one place to another without any time involved, we would teleport. We would be able to generate our body's frequency to vibrate at the appropriate frequency to transport it from where we are to where we desire to go. Just as the Bewitching family does, they pick where they want to go and with only a moment's thought about it are then there as Samantha waves her hands or snaps her fingers.

What I believe to know how our future selves, alien beings are doing now, teleporting as transportation, and the only reason that we would not see them is because we are still too limited in our expanding perception. So they are still invisible to us until we can expand our perception to tune them in. Just as a satellite signal, if we don't have the signal frequency, then we are not able to view the programming, simple as that.

Old Mortal Way of Believing about Death

The old way of death is to believe that our dear loved ones have died and we can only communicate with them mentally or through dreams, however how many really give absolute belief and validity to what they are doing? If you are then you are one step more evolved then others who do not. As the veils of illusion are becoming more transparent as they will the further along that we evolve, we will also change in the way we perceive other dimensions and even death.

New Bewitching Way of Knowing about Death

The new way will be that we will know that our loved ones have only shed their channel of this physical plane we still reside in. We will no longer just morn for them we will be in contact whenever we desire to. I can see in the future that we will even have a technology similar to a phone now that will able us to dial into the dimension that our loved one past into and call them and visually see each other as we converse in conversation. In the same way we do now when we call a loved one who lives two thousand miles away from our location to there location in our physical planet. The technology will advance to that level soon enough, all we have to do is take a look at the advances that thirty years ago seemed so impossible back then compared to now.

CRAFT 21

++++++++++++

APPRECIATION
USING SAMANTHA AS A ROLE MODEL

Appreciation is a high vibration of love. The highest energy of love that we know of on our planet so far. For many of us we can appreciate things when things or our experiences are going the way we want them to. But look out if things don't go the way we want or expected them to be. Why is that? It's because of our belief systems of memories that we became so habitual as a way of reacting for a long time. If you are reacting that way most of the time then it's a perfect opportunity to be aware so that these old beliefs systems can be transformed once and for all. It may take a lot of practice in the beginning just as anything we desire to change takes because we are still in the stages like Darrin. Having Samantha as a role model makes it easier because then we have the new idea's and knowledge to work with as we make the changes.

Let us look a little deeper in the way Darrin reacts whenever one of Samantha's relatives puts a spell on him. He reacts first with anger, frustration and sometimes some yelling with threats too. We know these are reactions of fear beliefs and energy and are the result of old ways that have become so habitually automatic. Darrin does not even give a second thought of how he is reacting. Then when we take notice of how Samantha responds most of the time, which is calmly mixed with love and appreciation we can clearly see the differences in comparison. Simply Darrin's reactions are of fear and Samantha's responses are of love.

We already know how different fear and love energy is, one will create stress the other will create a flow of calm and peacefulness. Though they are both energy they take on a different path of how our day and creations turn out as a result. And we also know the different vibrations of energy then affect the creation of our body too. So why would Darrin continue to react our of fear? All because he has not desired or been urged to become aware of the knowledge to consciously create the changes that are needed for the transformation.

So we can stay and be like Darrin and appreciation will not be experienced until we come to the end of the sometimes long path of appreciating when we experience the good out of any situation. Sometimes that can be a long time in waiting to appreciate and along the way in that waiting we also are affecting all of our creations along the way. Even thought it makes so much sense with all the benefits that responding as Samantha does in the love energy, it takes being aware and inserting the new loving way to respond as much as we can. Eventually it will also become habit for and take over the old habit as the old habit no longer is automatic because the new habit become automatic. Embedded in the new habit of responding loving comes appreciating everything along our path whether its good or not so good. Isn't that a way better higher benefit that will serve us through everything then all of the time. We sure can see that it's so worth it but if we allow the old beliefs and old automatic habits of reacting to continue, that is what creates it to seem harder then it really is to change or transform old to new ways.

So if we continue to use Samantha's role modeling and work on it throughout the day with everything, we will naturally allow it to become a great habit too. Then everything we go through will be seen its sparkling light of appreciation, everything. When we experience reality to not be what we want then its our opportunity to appreciate the learning lessons to transform it. To be gratefully appreciative that what we didn't want has been created by our self and we can now bring it to the neutral state of nothingness and recreate it with better thoughts. This will create more of what we want to experience in the process.

We then can see how being appreciate of everything really does create the difference in what we will be creating in our experiences with everyone and everything.

A Few Scenario's to Ponder

So you didn't get the job you wanted, appreciate it because there will always be another greater reason for not getting it. Later you may experience you received a better job with more money or a better job with less money but a job you'd prefer more then the one with better money.

You were late for work because you answered the phone on your way out, you didn't want to but you somehow followed your intuition maybe even without noticing it at the time. Through hindsight you see that if you didn't answer that phone call you may have been in the accident that occurred on your way to work, five minutes before you in the traffic jam.

Or you ate food that you later experienced food poisoning as a result. Oh yes you suffered but didn't take any medication for it and allowed your body to discard the toxins with diarrhea, The body took care of itself as it always has the ability to do when we allow it to do its natural divine working. You then can appreciate all you went through just to learn that your body can heal itself.

In one of the episodes when Samantha smelt a black Peruvian rose, her powers were affected by it. Darrin was all stressed out as usual but Samantha calmly with love accepted what occurred and learned from the experience. Darrin eventually did too, however he went through much more stress then Samantha because of his automatic reactions of fear. He tried to trust Aunt Clara, but even that took some adjusting to, yet Samantha could automatically trust Aunt Clara because she continues to respond with love and appreciation no matter what she is going through. Okay sometimes Samantha has little bits of anger, but not much compared to Darrin. Even when Samantha's uncle Arthur thinks it's so funny when he casts spells on Darrin, especially in one of the funniest episodes.

In the episode, uncle Arthur tells Darrin he knows a way Darrin can finally get back at Endora by using chanting and a blow horn while doing a little dance through the whole concoction. It makes me laugh, do you recall this episode? Just thinking how funny it looked when Darrin stood in front of Samantha and Endora as he did the spell and tried to make Endora disappear. When Samantha found her uncle Arthur laughing in the den, she didn't react as Darrin did later when he found out. Samantha just stood there not amused but not in a heat of anger either. She just stood there allowing her uncle to be who he was and accepted him but told him enough is enough. But of course uncle Arthur wouldn't listen until the Samantha, Darrin and Endora decided to teach him a lesson, Samantha still remained calm with accepting continued love and appreciation of the whole situation for all involved. This was blended with Samantha's love, appreciation, accepting and allowing all the others involved that she loved and the trust it would also work out too.

When we do this with everything in our own lives we will see all the reflection back to us how our life will transform too. Being in appreciation through everything is a gigantic leap compared to appreciating only when things are going good. It can become a daily habit in everything and if everyone became to be this way too, our planet would transform so amazingly we would truly see heaven on earth.

BEWTICHING MAGICAL POEMS

+++++++++++++

MODERN DAY SPELLS ARE AFFIRMATIONS

In our past lives we were burned at the stake
But never oh never did we give up our estates
Of powerful mind and being that we are
Nothing could stop us to unfold to be known
Of the beings of magic
Our heritage we hold

In the past we used the tools of spells and incantations to do
The magic that we always had in our being that was our truth
As times changed we created to sustain to elude
Modern day affirmations instead
Much more accepted and no longer tossed into the wind
We are always stronger then whence we began

Our bewitching unfolds
Into our knowing to own
Into a reality that proves
We are more then what we appeared
Of Darrin' s limits that always deceived
Of his rational conformity
Always trying to trick one's to believe
Instead we are like Samantha
Free to fly and do all we please
Because we never give up our infinite purpose
That powers our natural being

AnnaMarie Antoski

Zippity zap all possibilities become true
Just as twitching our noses
Or snapping our fingers
We can become more then what we were before
Blossoms of flowering
Our powers are intact
To be the craft that now never holds back

Expand and unfold into our destiny we call forth
Allowing the expansion to follow our own growth
Bewitched yet bewildered we may appear
We know our own kind
As we have thinned all the veils
To clearly be wise to never alter our divine
We broke the
Darrin's down
He has now resigned
Without all these controls
We are so free we as old illusion melt down

I AM FOR I AM I AFFIRM IT TO BE

I am powerful … I am indeed
Don't just look at the external
Go beyond this illusion past belief
Be the affirmation
Allow it to flow through
To see what is really powerfully true

All is just energy
Abbra cadabra ohm of the highest
There is magic for everyone to harness
Stir the brew of thoughts to become
Of any desire that is risen to know
It will be revealed when relaxation is felt
Into a trance of the powerful gap
Where all is one
You can feel it
Like a click of a switch
Our mind just connects
Our power is united with the absolute of the infinite

The stillness of the void
The power is released
Everything is possible
When we know it… into wisdom we retreat

It has been a daring adventure

and I am so glad you joined me.

Now that the final curtain is being drawn all the spells and illusions have been revealed, leaving you to choose to decide. Do you stay and be like Darrin or fly above on the leading edge and become like Endora, only you can decide.

Whatever you decide, allow it to be the most magically miraculously blissful experiences, so that all your paths are of the infinite source. That will always be the most beneficial in every way.

Infinitely AnnaMarie

Notes:

NOTES:

END NOTES, REFERENCES

Sia Baba
Website: http://www.saibaba.org/

Bashar, channeled by Darryl Anka
Website: http://www.bashar.org/

Gregg Braden
Website: http://www.greggbraden.com/

BTO, Beyond the Ordinary
Website: http://www.beyondtheordinary.net/

Tolly Burkan
Website: http://www.tollyburkan.com/

Tom Campbell
Website: http://www.my-big-toe.com/

Paul Dong
Website: http://www.pauldong.com/

Uri Geller
Website: http://site.uri-geller.com/

Burt Goldman
Website: http://www.burtgoldman.com/

Michio Kaku
Website: http://mkaku.org/

Bruce Lipton
Website: http://www.brucelipton.com/

Shirley McClaine
Website: http://www.shirleymaclaine.com/

Drunvalo Meichizekek
Website: http://www.drunvalo.net/

Greg Simmons
Website: http://www.physicsofchange.com/

News for the Soul, Nicole Whitney
Website: http://www.newsforthesoul.com/

Dr. Lee Pulos
Website: http://drpulos.com/

Ramtha, channeled by J. Z. Knight
Website: http://www.ramtha.com/

Thomas E. Raffill

Tony Robbins
Website: http://www.tonyrobbins.com/

Seth, channeled by Jane Roberts
Website: http://www.sethcenter.com/

Eckhart Tollie
Website: http://www.eckharttolle.com/

Mike Wright
Website: http://www.beyondtheordinary.net/mikewright.shtml

Wikipedia
Website: http://www.wikipedia.org/

Also by Annamarie Antoski

Infinite Manifesting

The Hidden Key Orgasm Reveals

Stumbling Through Infinity
Heart Reflection Poetry

Knowledge Transforms to Wisdom
Expanding Consciousness Poetry

ABOUT THE AUTHOR

AnnaMarie Antoski has studied the nature of reality for over 20 years with consistent passion and has integrated what she has learned into her life experiences. Sharing her self healing and psychic abilities she has become an inspiration in her field of experiences.

Website ... http://www.infinite-manifesting.org/